Understanding Christianity 1

Sue Penney

Heinemann

Heinemann Educational Publishers
Halley Court, Jordan Hill, Oxford OX2 8EJ
A Division of Reed Educational & Professional
Publishing Ltd

OXFORD MELBOURNE AUCKLAND
JOHANNESBURG BLANTYRE GABORONE
IBADAN PORTSMOUTH (NH) USA CHICAGO

First published 1997

01 00 99 98
10 9 8 7 6 5 4 3 2

British Library Cataloguing in Publication Data
A catalogue record for this book is available from the British Library

ISBN 0 435 36794 3

Designed and typeset by Artistix, Thame, Oxon
Illustrations by Diana Bowles
Photo research by Mags Robertson
Printed and bound in Spain by Mateu Cromo

Acknowledgements
The publishers would like to thank the following for permission to reproduce copyright material: HarperCollins Publishers Ltd for the Angelus, from *The Sunday Missal* on p.31; Methodist Publishing House for the Apostles' Creed, from *The Methodist Service Book*, 1975 on p.11; Kingsway's Thankyou Music for the extract taken from the song 'Be still for the Presence of the Lord' by D. J. Evans. Copyright © 1986 Kingsway's Thankyou Music, P.O. Box 75, Eastbourne, East Sussex BN23 6NT, UK. Used by kind permission of Kingsway's Thankyou Music on p.38. Quotations from the Bible used throughout the book are taken from *The Good News Bible*, published by the Bible Society/HarperCollins Publishers Ltd, UK © American Bible Society, 1966, 1971, 1976, 1992.

The publishers would like to thank the following for permission to use photographs: Andes Press Agency/Carlos Reyes-Manzo pp.26, 34 (both), 38, 42, 43, 47, 54, 56; Aspect Picture Library/Peter Carmichael p.12; Bridgeman Art Library/British Library p.48; J. Allan Cash Ltd. pp.10, 44, 45, 49; CIRCA Photo Library p.20; CIRCA Photo Library/Barrie Searle pp.14, 16; Collections p.32; Collections/Dorothy Burrows p.58; Collections/Geoff Howard pp.30 (right), 36; Collections/Brian Shuel p.59; James Davis Travel Photography p.28; Eye Ubiquitous/David Cumming p.33; Sonia Halliday and Laura Lushington p.18; Sonia Halliday Photographs pp.13, 17, 22; Sonia Halliday Photographs/Barry Searle p.24 (top); Images Colour Library p.23; Impact Photos p.39; Impact/Mohamed Ansar pp.8, 37; Impact/Mark Henley p.29; Magnum/Peter Marlow p.30 (left); Magnum Photographers/F. Mayer p.24 (bottom); Network/Barry Lewis p.21; Network/Homer Sykes p.55; Photofusion/Bob Watkins p.4; Ann & Bury Peerless pp.19; Jeff Price/Vince Owen/"The Image" pp.40, 41, 57; Rex Features p.46; Science Photo Library/Tony Hallas p.52; Frank Spooner Pictures/Tim O'Sullivan p.31; Frank Spooner Pictures/Uli Weyland p.60; Tony Stone Images pp.7, 9, 51; Trip/D. Burrows p.53; Zefa pp.15, 61.

Main front cover photo – Panos Pictures. Stained glass window on back and spine – Hutchison Library.

The publishers have made every effort to trace copyright holders. However, if any material has been incorrectly acknowledged, we would be pleased to correct this at the earliest opportunity.

Contents

Beliefs about God

1	Introduction to belief	4
2	So who needs God?	6
3	What Christians believe about God	8
4	What Christians believe – creeds	10

Beliefs about Jesus

5	Jesus' birth	12
6	Baptism and temptations	14
7	Friends to teach	16
8	Conflict with the authorities	18
9	The crucifixion	20
10	The Resurrection and Ascension	22
11	Jesus' teaching – parables	24
12	Jesus' teaching – miracles	26

The Christian Church

13	Outline of Church history	28
14	The Roman Catholic Church	30
15	The Orthodox Churches	32
16	The Anglican Churches	34
17	Other Protestant Churches	36
18	Christian worship	38
19	Different ways of worship	40
20	Signs and symbols used in worship	42
21	Church buildings – outside	44
22	Church buildings – inside	46

The Bible

23	History of the Bible	48
24	What's in the Bible?	50
25	The Creation story	52

Living as a Christian

26	Baptism	54
27	Confirmation	56
28	Festivals – Christmas	58
29	Festivals – Easter	60

Map and time chart	62
Glossary	63

1 Introduction to belief

What is belief?

Belief is a complicated idea. There is a lot of difference between knowing something and believing in it. The difference is that you can never prove something which you only believe. However, when you really believe something, you may feel sure that you are right. It feels like you know it. What some people know, other people can only believe. For example, if you live in the UK, you can know that snow is cold. You have touched it and felt it. But if you had always lived in a country where snow never falls, you could not know it for yourself. You would have to believe other people who told you that snow was cold.

What do people believe in?

Different people believe in different things. For example, children are taught to believe in Father Christmas and the tooth fairy. Most adults do not believe in them! Some people believe in 'luck'. They feel that seeing a black cat or touching a piece of wood is a way of making sure that things will go well for them. Breaking a mirror or walking under a ladder is seen as meaning that things will go wrong. Beliefs like these are called superstitions. Believing in superstitions often means that someone wants to have something to blame for things that have gone wrong.

You may believe that a pop group is brilliant. You study magazines that tell you about the stars in the group, put up posters on your bedroom walls and go to their concerts if you can. If you follow a football team, you find out as much as you can about the players, and travel to their matches whenever you can. Beliefs like this are often called hero-worship. Hero-worship of a pop star or a footballer can be shown in all sorts of ways. Fans may shout and clap, or scream and whistle. Some people wear the same clothes as their hero, or have their hair cut in the same way.

Hero-worship of a football team

These are all ways of showing that you believe the person is special. Hero-worship does not have to involve a stranger; it can be someone you know and really respect and try to be like.

Right or wrong?

When you are thinking about belief, it is important to remember that there is often no certain way of saying that someone is right or wrong. Even if you are the only person in the world who believes something, this may not stop you thinking you are right. Different people see things in different ways. The place and the way in which you have been brought up help to make you 'you'. People you know, things that have happened to you, even books you have read, may all cause you to see things in a particular way. People who believe in God may see things differently from someone who does not. People who belong to different religions may see things in different ways, too. Allowing people to have their own opinions, even if you disagree with them quite strongly, is an important part of being able to live with and get on with other people.

Why believe?

Everyone needs to believe in something. It may be just a belief that your team will win the Premier League, or it may be something more fundamental. Many people find that just being alive means they need to ask questions that can be very hard to answer. Why am I here? Is there a reason for living? How did the world begin? Disasters like floods or earthquakes make people ask questions about why the world seems such an unfair place. Bomb attacks or shootings cause people to ask why innocent people suffer. Trying to find answers to questions like these is part of growing up. This book is about people who have found answers in the religion called Christianity.

People see things in different ways. Do you see an old woman or a young woman in this picture?

Summing up

Everybody has to believe in something. Making up your own mind about important issues and allowing other people to make up theirs is an important part of growing up.

Activities

A

1 Look carefully at the picture on this page. How does it show that we cannot always say 'this is right' or 'this is wrong'?

2 How many superstitions can you list? Do you take notice of any of them in your life?

B

3 Work in pairs or small groups to think of as many things as you can that people believe in. Then try to say why you think people believe in them. (For example, believing in bad luck means they have something to blame when things go wrong.)

4 Make a list of things that are important to you (people, places, animals, objects). Write a few sentences about the most important of these things, explaining why it matters so much to you.

5 'I disagree with what you say, but I will defend completely your right to say it.' What do you think this means? Do you agree with it?

C

6 Look at newspapers or television news to find reports of one or two incidents that may cause people to ask questions about the meaning of life and why we are here. Write a short account of what you have read or seen. For each incident, include a few sentences saying what you think someone who has a strong religious belief would feel about it.

2 So who needs God?

'God is a very old man with a long white beard who lives up in the sky.'
Thomas, aged 6

'God is something people invented, because they are not strong enough to cope on their own.'
Lesley, aged 25

'God is the spirit who created everything. I believe he exists because I can't believe the universe and everything else happened by chance.'
Tony, aged 44

Picture language

'Picture language' is something we all use to describe things. We may describe someone greedy as 'a pig', or someone sly as 'a fox'. We do not expect anyone to believe that the person is really an animal, but saying things like this is a useful way of showing part of their character. Describing God is difficult, so people tend to use picture language. For example, God is often described as a person – a father or a king. Obviously this is not literally true; it would make God no more than a superhero whose power is limited to a physical body. But using terms like this for God does have a meaning. Saying he is a loving father tries to give the idea that God is someone who cares about people, and wants what is best for them. Saying he is a king is a way of trying to show how important and powerful he is. As you go through this book, try to remember that when people say things about God, they are often trying to put into words things that are very difficult to understand.

What is God?

Different religions teach about God in different ways. A religion which teaches that there is only one God is called **monotheistic**. Most monotheistic religions refer to God as 'he', even though they do not teach that God is male. Most teach that God is a **spirit** – in other words, that he does not have a body or physical form. He is therefore 'beyond' time or space. This means he is not limited by the same things that restrict human beings. This includes the belief that God is **eternal** – that is, that he was never born, and will never die. God is generally seen as a creator who cares about what he has created. For all this to be possible, God has to be all-knowing and all-powerful.

So who needs God?

At some times during our lives, most of us have feelings of wonder about the world. It may be when we are looking at something beautiful and powerful in nature, like a huge mountain range or the Niagara Falls. It may be something small and weak like a newborn baby. People who believe in God often say that sights or feelings like this are among the reasons why they believe that God exists.

In the quotes at the start of this unit, Tony said that he believes in God because he cannot believe that the world and everything in it began by chance. Many people feel that the amazing order of the universe and variety of life on earth means that there must be someone or something who designed it and decided how things should be. They feel that it strains belief too much to think that all this happened by chance. Other people reach the same conclusion for different reasons. They find that the idea of God is the only way in which they can make sense of the world. There is so much in the world that seems to be unfair and unjust, they feel a need to look beyond the world itself to try to see a pattern or meaning behind things.

Beautiful scenery inspires wonder

Activities

A

1 Think of three examples of how you might use 'picture language' in your life. How does it help you to explain what someone or something is like?

2 Religions which teach that there is only one God, teach similar things about what God is like. What do they teach? Make sure you explain the technical words.

B

3 Why do you think most religions teach about God as if he were male?

4 Things that are beautiful or powerful can make people think about God. Make a list of things you can think of in the world that might cause people to believe that God exists. Then make another list of things that might cause people to say that he does not exist. Choose one item from either list, and draw a picture of it.

5 Working in small groups, think of as many reasons as you can why people might say that they believe in God. Write down the five most important reasons.

C

6 Imagine you had been asked for your opinion about God to put at the beginning of this unit. What would you have written?

Summing up

There are many reasons why people believe in God. Some of them are difficult to express in words. This does not make them any less important.

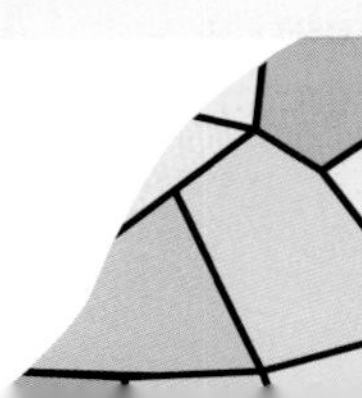

3 What Christians believe about God

Christianity is the most widely held religious belief in the world. There are about 1800 million people around the world who claim to be Christians. They are divided into thousands of different groups. Some groups have millions of members, others have only a few dozen. Not all the groups and individuals share exactly the same beliefs. This unit looks at belief in God, which is the basis of the Christian faith.

Belief in God

Christians believe that there is one God. They believe that God can be understood in three persons: God the Father, God the Son and God the Holy Spirit. This belief that God is three yet only one is called the **Trinity**. It is a complicated but important part of Christian teaching about God.

God the Father

For Christians, God the Father is a spirit who is eternal, and the creator of the universe. He is seen as a loving father who cares about what he has made. Christians believe that all through history God has chosen special people to tell others what he is like. They believe that the best and most complete demonstration of what God is like came through a man whom they believe was God's Son.

God the Son

Christians believe that God the Son was a man who lived in Palestine (modern-day Israel) 2000 years ago. His name was Jesus. Christians often call him Jesus **Christ**. Although it is often used as if it was part of Jesus' name, Christ is a special title. It comes from the Greek word *Christos*. This is a translation of the **Hebrew** word ***Messiah***. Hebrew is the language of the Jews, and Jesus was a Jew.

Christians at a church in London

At the time of Jesus, Jews were waiting for God to send a Messiah who would begin the kingdom of God on earth. Christians believe that Jesus was this Messiah.

Christians believe that Jesus had a special relationship with God. They believe that he was both completely God and completely man. This means that through the life and teachings of Jesus, Christians can see what God is like. The death of Jesus is especially important for Christians. They believe that Jesus died when he was **crucified**, but two days later he came back to life. This is called the **Resurrection**. For Christians, the Resurrection shows that death is not the end. They believe that the death and Resurrection of Jesus changed for ever the relationship between God and human beings. Because Jesus died, it is possible for **sins** to be forgiven.

Sin is a word that describes all wrong-doing which puts up barriers between people and God. Forgiveness of sins is an important part of Christian teaching and is the reason why Christians often call Jesus their Saviour. They believe he has saved them from the results of their sins, which stopped them getting close to God.

God the Holy Spirit

Christians believe that the Holy Spirit is the power of God working in the world today. He cannot be seen, but Christians believe that they can see his effect in their lives and in the lives of other people. They believe that the Spirit's power makes it possible to worship God. The Spirit also gives them power to live their lives in the way that God wants.

The force behind waves cannot be seen

Summing up

Christian beliefs about God are the most important part of their faith.

Activities

A

1 Why do Christians call Jesus 'Christ'?

2 Why do Christians call Jesus 'Saviour'?

B

3 Some people have tried to explain the Trinity by using the example of a shamrock or clover leaf. Draw a leaf like this, and try to describe why it might help to explain what the Trinity is like.

4 Explain as carefully as you can what Christians believe about Jesus.

5 Christians believe in Jesus' Resurrection. What does this mean? Why is the death and Resurrection of Jesus so important for Christians?

C

6 Christians say that they cannot see the Holy Spirit, but they can feel his effect. Think of two other examples that involve forces which you can only know by the effect they have.

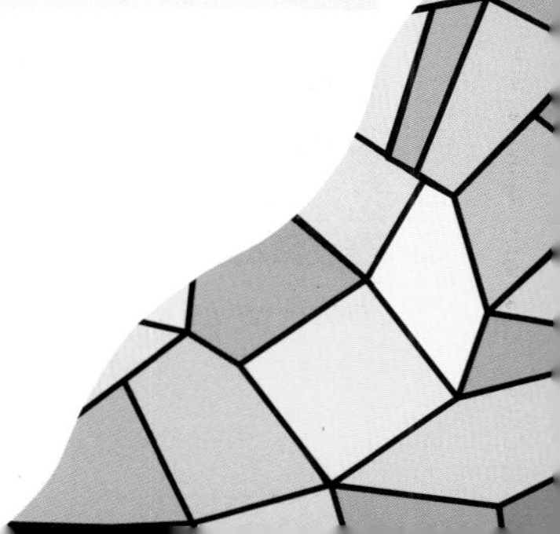

4 What Christians believe – creeds

The word **creed** comes from the Latin word *credere*, which means to believe. Christian creeds are statements that sum up the most important things that Christians believe.

Why are creeds needed?

Christianity did not begin with a complete set of beliefs. Early Christians had to work out what they believed as people asked questions about the new faith. As Christianity developed, more detailed and so more complicated statements of faith were needed.

For example, Jesus and all his first followers were Jews. The most important teaching of **Judaism** is that there is only one God. The early Christians all believed this. Yet they were convinced that Jesus was God, too. How was this possible? They began calling Jesus 'Son of God', but this in itself needed explaining.

Antakya (Antioch) in Turkey today. Many early Christians lived here

How was it possible for God to have a son? Had the Son always been there? Was he really a man? Was he really God? Could he be both? It took years and many discussions between important Christian leaders before statements of belief about this and other important questions were agreed.

Most Christian creeds go back to the first few hundred years of Christianity. This was a time when Christianity was growing very quickly. A creed was an important way of summing up the faith, so that people could know what it involved. It was also a way of making sure that false teachings were not being accepted. Creeds are still used in **worship** today, when Christians repeat them to share what they believe about God.

The first creed

The first creed was a simple statement of faith in Jesus – 'Jesus is Lord'. This is still the most important part of Christian belief. A lord is someone who has power or authority over other people, so this is a way for Christians to say that Jesus is the most important thing in their life.

The Apostles' Creed

The **Apostles'** Creed was given this name because it sums up what the first Christians taught. Apostle is a name that is sometimes used for the first followers of Jesus. The Apostles' Creed was probably not written down until about the third century CE, but the teachings it contains are much older than that. The first section contains beliefs about God. The second section contains beliefs about Jesus. The third section is about other teachings of Christianity. Notice that some words are used in a special way. For example, 'holy Catholic Church' means a Church that includes everyone; it does not just refer to the Roman Catholic Church. 'Communion of saints' means fellowship of all Christians.

The Apostles' Creed

I believe in God, the Father Almighty,
creator of heaven and earth.

I believe in Jesus Christ, his only Son,
our Lord,
He was conceived by the power of the
Holy Spirit
And born of the Virgin Mary.
He suffered under Pontius Pilate,
was crucified, died and was buried.
He descended to the dead.
On the third day he rose again.
He ascended into heaven,
and is seated at the right hand of the
Father.
He will come again to judge the living
and the dead.

I believe in the Holy Spirit,
the holy Catholic Church,
the communion of saints,
the forgiveness of sins,
the resurrection of the body,
and the life everlasting.

The Nicene Creed

Another important creed is the Nicene Creed, which is named after a meeting of church leaders that took place in a city called Nicaea in 325 CE. This is more detailed than the Apostles' Creed, because it was intended to clear up misunderstandings in what some Christians were teaching at the time.

Summing up

Creeds are important statements of belief. Many Christians find it helpful to know that they are repeating words which sum up what Christians have been believing and saying for hundreds of years.

Activities

A

1 Explain what a creed is. Why did creeds begin?

2 Why do you think repeating creeds is still important in Christian worship today?

B

3 What does 'Jesus is Lord' mean? Explain why a simple statement like this was not enough to sum up the beliefs of later Christians.

4 Find out what the word apostle means. Why do you think Jesus' first followers were given this name?

5 Try to sum up the most important things in your life. What would you choose? Write about them, or you could choose to draw a picture that shows the things.

C

6 Write a summary of the Apostles' Creed in your own words.

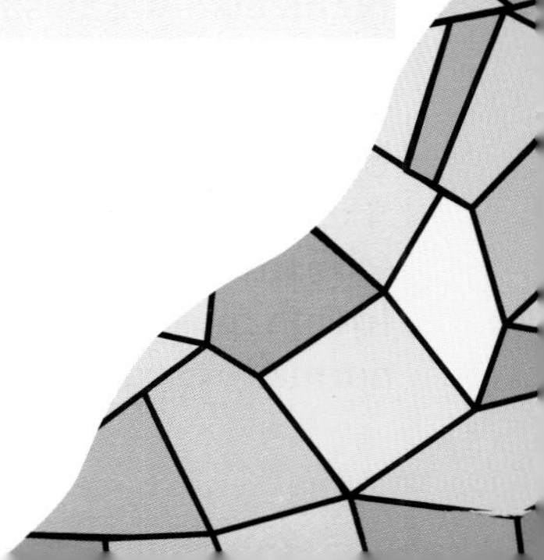

5 Jesus' birth

Most of the information that we have about Jesus comes from the Bible, the Christian holy book. The part of the Bible which tells of the life of Jesus is called the **Gospels**. The Gospels were written by followers of Jesus, and they are more than just accounts of his life. Only two of the Gospel writers (Matthew and Luke) include the birth of Jesus in their Gospels.

The story of the birth of Jesus has been told over and over again for 2000 years. In that time, many details have been added. This means that things which most people expect to be included in the story are not in the Bible. For example, the Gospels do not include a stable, or animals watching. Matthew mentions wise men from the East coming to see Jesus, but he says that they brought three gifts, not that there were three men. There is no suggestion that they were kings.

A street in Nazareth today

The birth of Jesus

Luke's Gospel makes it clear that Jesus was not an ordinary baby. His mother, Mary, had been told by an angel that she would have a baby and should call him Jesus. At the time when the baby was due to be born, the Romans ordered a census, a count of the population. For this, everyone had to go back to the place where their families originally came from. Mary and her husband Joseph had to travel from their home in Nazareth to a town called Bethlehem in the south of Palestine. This is why Jesus was born in Bethlehem.

Because of the census, accommodation in Bethlehem was in short supply, and Mary and Joseph could not find anywhere to stay. No one really knows where Jesus was born, but Luke says the new baby was laid in a manger. A manger is a feeding trough for animals, so many people have thought that Mary and Joseph must have been somewhere that was normally used for keeping animals. However, in those days, animals often shared part of the house with people, so it does not necessarily mean that they were in a 'cowshed'. One thing that is clear is that Jesus was born in a place where the people were very poor.

Luke says that shepherds looking after their sheep in the fields outside the town were the first to learn of the baby's birth. They were told by angels. In those days, shepherds were thought to be inferior and were looked down on. Luke mentions them to emphasise that Jesus' birth was important for everyone.

Matthew includes the wise men visiting Jesus. This cannot have happened at the time of his birth. The wise men travelled hundreds of kilometres, a journey that would have taken time to prepare for, and many months to complete. The Gospel says that they 'came to the house where the young child was'.

It seems likely that for some reason Mary and Joseph had decided to stay in Bethlehem after the census. The wise men thought that the star they had been following was announcing the birth of a king, and so they went first to the king's palace. King Herod the Great was very afraid of a rival. After he had seen the wise men, he ordered that every male child in Bethlehem under the age of two should be killed. Mary and Joseph were warned in a dream that this would happen, and they escaped to Egypt – the nearest place where Herod had no authority.

When was Jesus born?

It is impossible to give an exact date on which Jesus was born. Although the years in the Western calendar are supposed to start at the year of Jesus' birth, the numbers cannot be accurate. For example, the Bible says that Jesus was born in the reign of King Herod the Great, who ordered the killing of babies under the age of two. Roman records show that Herod died in 4 BCE. Other records show that in 7 BCE the planets Jupiter and Saturn came together, something that happens only once every 805 years. In February in 6 BCE Mars moved past them, making a triangle in the sky. Rare events like this would have been noticed, and they may be an explanation of the 'star' the wise men followed. It seems most likely, therefore, that Jesus was born around 6 BCE.

The Grotto of the Nativity in Bethlehem

Summing up

The writers of the Gospels wanted to make it clear that they were telling the story of the birth of a very special baby.

Activities

A

1 How many ways can you find in which the Gospel writers show they thought they were writing about the birth of a special baby? (It may help you to look up the stories in the Bible – Matthew's Gospel chapters 1 and 2 and Luke chapter 2.)

2 How can we tell that the wise men cannot have visited Jesus as soon as he was born?

B

3 Using a Bible to help you, write your own version of the story of the birth of Jesus. You could illustrate it, too.

4 Shepherds were very poor, and the wise men were obviously rich. Why do you think the Gospel writers included these two groups in their story?

5 Explain why Herod ordered that baby boys in Bethlehem under the age of two should be killed.

C

6 How many reasons can you think of why it is difficult to date the birth of Jesus exactly?

6 Baptism and temptations

Jesus in the Temple

There is only one story in the Bible about the childhood of Jesus. It is in Luke's Gospel. It says that when Jesus was twelve years old, he went with Mary and Joseph to Jerusalem. They were going to the Jewish festival of Passover. When Mary and Joseph were ready to go home, Jesus was not with them. In those days people travelled in large groups for fear of robbers. Mary and Joseph must have thought that Jesus was with other people in the group. When they discovered he was missing, they rushed back to Jerusalem, and spent three days looking for him. When they found him, he was in the **Temple**. This was the most important building in the Jewish religion. Jesus was talking to the leaders of the religion. When Mary asked if he had not realized they would be worried, he said, 'Didn't you know I would be in my father's house?' This was not the way Jews usually talked about God. This story shows that even as a child, Jesus knew there was something special about his relationship with God.

Apart from this story, nothing is known of the early life of Jesus. Luke's Gospel says that he grew up in Nazareth with Mary and Joseph. In those days, all men learned a trade, and it seems likely that Joseph taught Jesus his own trade as a carpenter.

John the Baptist

When Jesus was about 30 years old, a man named John began preaching in Palestine. He told the Jews that they should **repent** – be sorry for all the things they had done wrong. To show that they were sorry, they should be baptized. **Baptism** is a special ceremony to wash away sin. Because of the way John was preaching, some Jews began to wonder if he was the Messiah they were hoping for, but he said he was not. He said that another man was coming who was greater than him. This man would be the Messiah.

The River Jordan today

Jesus' baptism

As John was preaching one day, Jesus joined the crowd and asked John to baptize him. The Gospels make it clear that John recognized Jesus as the man he had been waiting for. At first, John refused to baptize him, because he said that Jesus should be the one to baptize *him*. When Jesus insisted, however, John baptized him. The Gospels say that as Jesus came up out of the water, God's spirit came down like a dove, and a voice said, 'You are my own dear son, I am pleased with you.' They do not say that anyone else saw or heard this. It probably means that because he had been baptized, Jesus became sure of the work that God wanted him to do.

Jesus' temptations

After his baptism, Jesus spent some time on his own. He went into the desert. This was an area where very little grew, so there were not likely to be other people around. Jesus needed to spend time on his own so that he could think and pray about the work he was going to do.

The Bible says that while he was there he was tempted by the Devil three times. When the Bible was written, people had no doubt that the Devil was a real being. Some people still believe this, and believe that Jesus was visited by this being who talked to him. Other people today believe that 'devil' is really picture language for describing a force of evil in the world, rather than a real person. However they came, the three temptations were obviously real to Jesus. The temptations were all about the right way to use the power that God had given him. The temptations were:

- to turn stones into bread
- to throw himself off the top of a tall tower, so that God would send angels to save him
- to make himself a great king, and rule lots of countries.

If Jesus had done any of these things, it would have forced people to believe in him. However, Jesus rejected them all. He felt that force was not what God wanted. He spent 40 days in the desert. At the end of that time, Jesus knew how he was going to do God's work.

Jesus went to the desert to be alone

Summing up

Christians believe that all of Jesus' life before he began teaching was spent preparing for the work God wanted him to do.

Activities

A

1 What reasons can you give why there is so little information about the first 30 years of Jesus' life?

2 Explain why Jesus' baptism was such an important event.

B

3 Look up the story in the Bible of when Jesus became lost as a child. (Luke chapter 2, verses 41–51). What does the story show about what Jesus was like as a child?

4 Why do you think John refused at first to baptize Jesus? Why do you think that Jesus insisted on being baptized?

5 What were the temptations of Jesus? Why did he reject them all?

C

6 Make up a story about being tempted to do something which you felt was wrong. What happened? Describe what your feelings were.

7 Friends to teach

Disciples

After Jesus had been baptized and tempted, it seems likely that he worked with John the Baptist for a time. They baptized people in the River Jordan, telling them they should repent of the things they had done wrong. In those days, it was not unusual for religious teachers to have groups of followers. People would come when they could, and go back to their homes and jobs when they needed to. Someone who followed a teacher like this was often called a **disciple**. Disciple is a word that means 'someone who learns'.

Then John was arrested and put in prison. News had reached the king, Herod Antipas, that John had been telling people that the way the king was living was against the laws of God. The king was angry. As a friend of John's, it would have been dangerous for Jesus to stay, so he left the River Jordan and went back to his home area of Galilee. This is the beginning of the work that Christians call Jesus' **ministry** – the three years he spent preaching and teaching before he was killed.

Lake Galilee

For most of the time he was preaching, Jesus was followed by large crowds. Like the crowds at the River Jordan, they must have been people who came when their responsibilities at home and at work allowed. At the beginning of his ministry, Jesus seems to have felt that he needed special friends and helpers who would be with him all the time. This account in Mark's Gospel tells how Jesus called the first of them to be his followers.

Jesus calls four fishermen

After John had been put in prison, Jesus went to Galilee and preached the Good News from God. 'The right time has come,' he said, 'and the Kingdom of God is near!' Turn away from your sins and believe the Good News!'

As Jesus walked along the shore of Lake Galilee, he saw two fishermen, Simon and his brother Andrew, catching fish with a net. Jesus said to them, 'Come with me, and I will teach you to catch men.' At once they left their nets and went with him. He went a little farther on and saw two other brothers, James and John, the sons of Zebedee. They were in their boat getting their nets ready. As soon as Jesus saw them, he called them; they left their father Zebedee in the boat with the hired men and went with Jesus.

(Mark 1, 16–20)

Fishing boats on Lake Galilee today

Some time later, Jesus chose these four men, together with another eight men, to be apostles. Apostle comes from a Greek word which means 'someone who is sent out' – in other words, a messenger. Jesus said to them, 'I have chosen you to be with me, I will also send you out to preach,' (Mark 3, 14). They were to be his closest followers. Later on they were to be the ones that he sent out with authority to preach and heal.

Why did Jesus choose disciples?

The key to Jesus' need for disciples is given in the beginning of the quotation from the Bible on the opposite page. 'The right time has come and the Kingdom of God is near!' Jesus' preaching is all about bringing people closer to the Kingdom of God. In order to do this, he needed to have 'apprentices' who would learn from him and who could then go out and teach others, especially when Jesus himself was no longer able to preach.

Summing up

Jesus' disciples were men who were chosen to learn from him and then go out and spread his teachings.

Activities

A

1 What does the word ministry mean? Why did Jesus need people to help him?

2 Why did Jesus not carry on John's work after John was arrested?

B

3 What does disciple mean? What does apostle mean? Explain what Jesus was asking the men to do.

4 What do you think Jesus meant when he said that he would teach Simon and Andrew 'to catch men'?

5 Why did Jesus need followers? Explain the difference between the people who followed Jesus when they could, and the disciples.

C

6 Imagine you were watching as Jesus called either Simon and Andrew or James and John to follow him. Write a description of what happened, and how you felt about it.

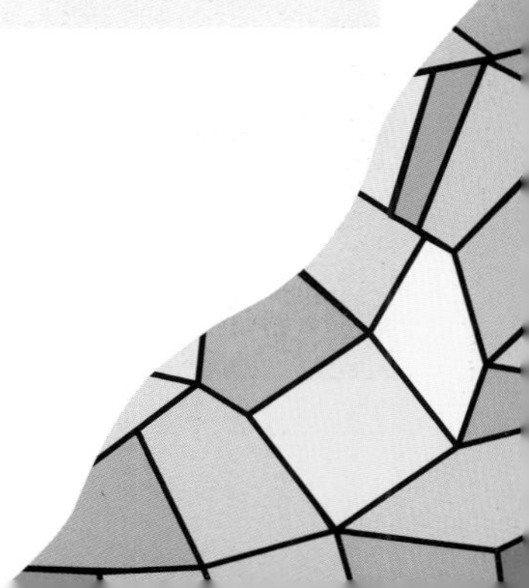

8 Conflict with the authorities

Background

In the first century CE, Palestine was a very unhappy country. It was ruled by the Romans, whom most Jews hated. They had taken over the Jews' country, and they were **Gentiles** (non-Jews). No good Jew at the time would even talk to a Gentile if they could avoid it. The Romans allowed Jews to continue worshipping God in their own way, but there were strict rules. Taxes had to be paid, soldiers had to be obeyed, and there had to be complete obedience to Roman law. Many of the leaders of Judaism (the Jewish religion) spent much of their time struggling to keep a balance between obeying the rules of their religion, and not upsetting the Romans to whom they owed their power.

The authorities and leaders of the country were based in the capital city, Jerusalem. Most of Jesus' teaching took place in Galilee, the area in the north of the country where he had been brought up. But the leaders had obviously heard of Jesus. The more they heard, the more alarmed they became. He did not always say things of which the Jewish leaders approved. He frequently said things of which they did not approve. He criticized them! He was popular with ordinary people, and huge crowds often followed him to listen to his preaching. There were even rumours among the people that Jesus might be the Messiah. All Jews at the time were hoping that God was going to send a leader who would drive out the Romans and begin a new kingdom of God. Jesus' actions did not fit what the leaders were expecting a Messiah to be like. For the leaders, Jesus was dangerous!

Palm Sunday

The crisis came when Jesus and his friends travelled to Jerusalem for the Festival of the Passover. Jesus chose to enter the city riding on a donkey. A crowd gathered, and began throwing down their cloaks and branches from the trees by the side of the road for the donkey to walk on. This was a sign of respect for a leader – rather like a red carpet today. The people shouted, 'God bless him who comes in the name of the Lord!' In other words, they were showing that they thought Jesus was the Messiah.

The ruins of a synagogue in Capernaum in Palestine. Jesus preached in a synagogue on this site

Clearing the Temple

After he had entered Jerusalem, Jesus went to the Temple. The Temple was the most important building in the Jewish religion. It was a splendid building, made of gold and marble. It was built like a series of squares, one inside the next. The outermost square was called the Court of the Gentiles. Many non-Jews were interested in the Jewish religion, and this was the only part of the Temple they were allowed to enter. However, the Court of the Gentiles had been taken over by people who were changing money and selling animals for **sacrifice**. At that time, killing an animal so that its life could be given to God was an important part of Jewish worship. Only animals bought in the Temple were allowed to be sacrificed, and special Temple money had to be used to buy them and to offer as gifts. The Court of the Gentiles was more like a market than a place of worship. To make things worse, the men who did the buying and selling were known to charge high prices and to cheat the people.

Jesus saw what was happening in the Temple, and he was angry. He told the people that in the Jewish Scriptures – the holy books – God says, 'My Temple shall be called a house of prayer.' But he said, 'You have turned it into a hideout for thieves.' Then he turned over all the traders' stalls. All the people were amazed. The leaders of Judaism made up their minds. Jesus had to be got rid of!

This model shows the Temple at the time of Jesus

Summing up

Jesus' preaching and his popularity made it certain that he would come into conflict with the Jewish authorities.

Activities

A

1 Explain why the authorities were afraid of Jesus.

2 Why do you think Jesus was angry when he saw what was happening in the Temple?

B

3 Explain why the Jews did not get on with the Romans.

4 What happened on Palm Sunday? Why was this so important?

5 Why do you think Jesus was so angry when he went into the Temple? What do his actions tell you about him?

C

6 Find out more about the Temple at the time of Jesus – what it looked like and how it was used. Working on your own or in small groups, prepare an information sheet that could be used to tell younger children about the Temple. Don't forget, young children need pictures!

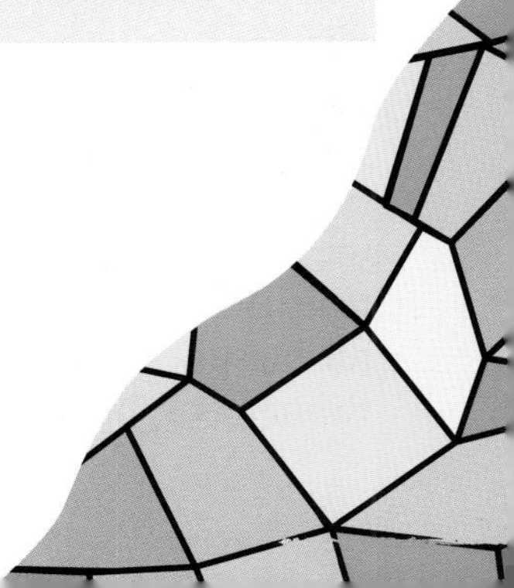

9 The crucifixion

After he had cleared the Temple, Jesus spent three days teaching people. The authorities were looking for a chance to arrest him, but they did not dare risk a riot by trying to arrest him when he was surrounded by so many people. At night, Jesus stayed with friends in a village outside the city.

At the end of the week, it was the Jewish festival of Passover. The most important part of the festival is the Passover meal. Jesus arranged to eat this with his closest friends, his disciples. It was the last meal he ate with them, and so Christians often call it the Last Supper. It is the meal that is remembered in the church service called the **Eucharist** or **Holy Communion**.

This painting of the Last Supper comes from Africa

The arrest of Jesus

After the meal was over, Jesus and the disciples went to a quiet place just outside the city. It was called Garden of Gethsemane, which means the garden of the olive press. One of Jesus' disciples, Judas Iscariot, 'tipped off' the authorities that this would be a good time to arrest him. No one really knows why Judas did this. It may have been because he was paid 30 pieces of silver – a lot of money at that time. It could have been that Judas thought that if Jesus was arrested and in danger he would be forced to show his power.

As Jesus was praying in the Garden, soldiers came and arrested him. He was taken in front of a meeting of the highest Jewish court, called the **Sanhedrin**. They asked him if he was the Messiah. The Gospels give slightly different accounts of what Jesus said, but they all agree that he refused to deny it. For the Jews, this was **blasphemy**. Blasphemy comes from a word that means 'evil-speaking'. It means saying something about God that is not true. According to Jewish law, the punishment for blasphemy was death. However, under Roman law, only the Romans had the right to order that anyone should die. To be sentenced, Jesus had to be taken to the Roman governor, a man called Pontius Pilate. The Sanhedrin did not expect Pilate to be very impressed by being told that Jesus was guilty of blasphemy against the Jewish God, so they 'translated' it. They said that Jesus called himself a king. As the person in charge of keeping the peace, Pilate could not ignore the possible threat to Roman law. He ordered that Jesus should be crucified.

The crucifixion

Crucifixion was a common Roman method of execution. It involved being nailed or tied to a wooden cross. It is one of the most cruel ways ever known of killing people. The victims were usually whipped or tortured beforehand, and so they were already weak. They eventually died because they lacked the strength to breathe, but it could take days before this happened.

Jesus was crucified on the Friday morning, on a hill just outside the city of Jerusalem. Two thieves were crucified there at the same time. Jesus died in the afternoon. When he was dead his disciples asked for, and were given, permission to take the body down from the cross, and bury it. This had to be done quickly, because at sunset the Jewish **Sabbath** began. Sabbath is the Jewish holy day, when work – which includes carrying anything – is forbidden. The usual place to bury a body was in a cave in the rock. Jesus' body was placed in a cave, and the entrance was closed with a large stone.

The Gospels make it clear that the disciples were heartbroken. They had hoped that Jesus was a great leader, and was going to begin a new kingdom. Instead, he had died like a thief. It was the end of everything they had hoped for. They were also very afraid that as his friends their own lives were in danger.

This Easter procession follows the route that Jesus took on his way to be crucified

Summing up

Jesus was arrested on the Thursday, put on trial overnight, and crucified by the Romans on the Friday.

Activities

A

1 What do Christians call the Passover meal that Jesus ate with his disciples? Why is it important?

2 Why were the disciples in a hurry to take Jesus' body down from the cross?

B

3 Why did the authorities not dare to arrest Jesus when he was teaching in the Temple?

4 What does blasphemy mean? Explain why the Jewish authorities changed the accusation against Jesus before they took him to Pilate.

5 Read Matthew chapter 26, verses 14–16 and chapter 27, verses 3–5. What possible reasons can you suggest for why Judas acted as he did?

C

6 Work in pairs to make up a conversation which could have taken place between two of the disciples on the evening of the Friday on which Jesus died. Act it out for the rest of your group.

10 The Resurrection and Ascension

Jesus had been crucified and buried on the Friday. Early on the Sunday morning, some of his women friends went to his tomb. They wanted to **anoint** his body with oil and spices. This was what usually happened to the body of someone who had died, but the women had not been able to do it before because it counted as work, which is forbidden on the Sabbath. When they got to the tomb, the stone which had sealed the entrance had been moved. There was no sign of the body.

The Gospels have slightly different accounts of what happened next, but they agree that the women were told by one or two men wearing white (Matthew calls them angels) that Jesus had come back to life. The women were terrified, and rushed off to tell the other disciples what they had seen. According to Luke's Gospel, the men did not believe what they were told. Two of the disciples ran to the tomb and found that it was all exactly as the women had said – the cloth in which Jesus' body had been wrapped was still there, but there was no sign of his body. All the Gospels agree that later that day and over the next few weeks the disciples saw Jesus several times.

This is like the tomb in which Jesus was buried

What happened at the Resurrection?

No one really understands what happened at the Resurrection. The Gospels present it as a fact that Jesus came back to life. They do not even try to explain it. On the occasions he met the disciples afterwards, the Gospels are clear that Jesus did not have a normal human body. They describe how he could be in more than one place at the same time, and how he appeared in rooms where all the doors were locked. However, he also ate and drank with the disciples to show that he was not a ghost.

Many people have put forward different ideas about how these things might have happened. One of the most common 'explanations' is that it was not really Jesus who was crucified. Another is that it *was* Jesus who died, but the disciples hid the body and invented the story of the Resurrection. Other people think that Jesus was not really dead when he was taken down from the cross, and he recovered from his injuries in the tomb.

Christians say that none of these ideas explain the change that took place in the disciples after the Resurrection. Something changed them from being frightened, ordinary people into men who spent the rest of their lives preaching about Jesus. Many of them risked their lives and in the end died for what they believed.

Most Christians would say that the Resurrection was an event that really happened. Just because it is not possible to explain it does not mean that it did not happen. They believe that the Resurrection was a **miracle** – something that shows God's power but which cannot be explained. They say that nothing like the Resurrection ever happened before or since.

The Ascension

The last occasion Jesus' disciples saw him is called the **Ascension**. The Gospels say that Jesus gave the disciples instructions about how they were to carry on his preaching. He promised that although he was not going to be with them, he would send a 'helper'. Christians believe that this helper is the Holy Spirit. No one is really sure what happened then. The Bible says that 'a cloud hid him from their sight'. Some people believe that this means Jesus was lifted up into the sky in some amazing way. Other people prefer to believe that he walked away up the mountain.

The Mount of Olives is where the Ascension took place

Summing up

Believing that Jesus rose from the dead is the most important part of Christian teaching.

Activities

A **1** Why were the women going to the tomb on the Sunday morning?

2 What did Jesus promise the disciples at the Ascension? Why do Christians think that this is so important?

B **3** How many reasons can you think of why the disciples might not have believed what the women were telling them?

4 What possible explanations are there for what might have happened at the Resurrection? What do you think is the most likely explanation?

5 Why are Christians so sure that after the Resurrection Jesus was not a ghost?

C **6** How do you think the disciples felt after the Ascension? Try to explain how this compares with what they felt after the Crucifixion.

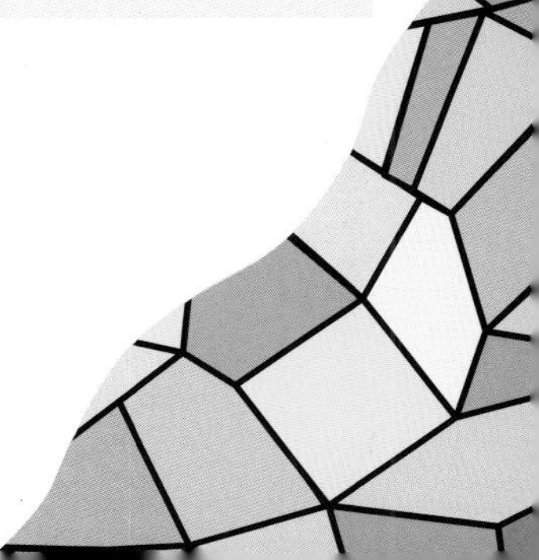

11 *Jesus' teaching – parables*

When Jesus was teaching, he often used **parables** to make the lesson clear. A parable is a story that includes a meaning. Stories are interesting to listen to, and they are more likely to be remembered than just giving people instructions about how they should live.

The parables of the lost sheep and the lost coin are a pair of stories that teach the same lesson. Like many of the stories Jesus told, they grew out of the situation he was in. People had come to listen to Jesus teach. Many of them were the sort of people of whom the **Pharisees** (religious leaders) did not approve. Jesus wanted to show that God cares for everyone.

The parables of the lost sheep and the lost coin

One day when many tax collectors and other outcasts came to listen to Jesus, the Pharisees and the teachers of the Law started grumbling. 'This man welcomes outcasts and even eats with them!' So Jesus told them this parable:

'Suppose one of you has 100 sheep and loses one of them – what does he do? He leaves the other 99 sheep in the pasture, and goes looking for the one that he lost until he finds it. When he finds it he is so happy that he puts it on his shoulders and carries it back home. Then he calls his friends and neighbours together and says to them, "I am so happy I found my lost sheep. Let us celebrate." In the same way, I tell you, there will be more joy in heaven over one sinner who repents than over 99 respectable people who did not need to repent.

Or suppose a woman who has ten silver coins loses one of them – what does she do? She lights a lamp, sweeps her house and looks carefully until she finds it. When she finds it she calls her friends and neighbours together and says to them, "I am so happy I found the coin I lost. Let us celebrate!" In the same way, I tell you, the angels of God rejoice over one sinner who repents.'

Luke 15, 1–11

A shepherd in Israel today

The silver coins in the story would have come from the woman's wedding headdress

The parable of the unforgiving servant

Once there was a king who decided to check on his servants' accounts. He had just begun to do so when one of them was brought in who owed him millions of pounds. The servant did not have enough to pay his debt, so the king ordered him to be sold as a slave, with his wife and his children and all that he had, in order to pay the debt. The servant fell on his knees before the king. 'Be patient with me,' he begged, 'and I will pay you everything.' The king felt sorry for him so he forgave him the debt and let him go.

Then the man went out and met one of his fellow servants who owed him a few pounds. He grabbed him and started choking him. 'Pay back what you owe me!' he said. His fellow servant fell down and begged him, 'Be patient with me, and I will pay you back!' But he refused. Instead he had him thrown into jail until he should pay the debt. When the other servants saw what had happened, they went to the king and told him everything. So he called the servant in. 'You worthless slave!' he said. 'I forgave you the whole amount you owed me, just because you asked me to. You should have had mercy on your fellow servant, just as I had mercy on you.' The king was very angry, and he sent the servant to jail to be punished until he should pay back the whole amount. And Jesus concluded, 'That is how my father in heaven will treat every one of you unless you forgive your brother from your heart.'

Matthew 18, 21–25

In the parable of the unforgiving servant, Jesus was teaching the lesson that everyone needs to be forgiven for things they have done wrong. So everyone needs to forgive other people, too. It was another way of teaching the lesson that you should treat other people as you would like to be treated yourself.

Summing up

Jesus used parables to teach lessons in a way that would be easy to remember.

Activities

A

1. What lesson was Jesus trying to teach in the parables of the lost sheep and the lost coin?
2. What lesson was Jesus trying to teach in the parable of the unforgiving servant?

B

3. Explain as carefully as you can why Jesus taught in parables.
4. Why did the Pharisees not approve of many of the people who had come to listen to Jesus?
5. What do you think of the behaviour of the first servant in the parable of the unforgiving servant? What do you think of the behaviour of the king?

C

6. Working in groups of at least three, make up a short play about the unforgiving servant to act out. Try to think of some way to make the lesson of the story clear.

12 *Jesus' teaching – miracles*

A miracle is something that cannot be understood, and which seems to be outside the normal laws of life. The men who wrote the Gospels included the stories of Jesus working miracles because they used them as signs. They wanted to show that Jesus had special power, which came from God. This power was not something that ordinary people shared.

Why did Jesus work miracles?

There are many reasons why Jesus worked miracles. Sometimes it seems that when people believed in him, he did not want to let them down. On other occasions he worked miracles to prove that he meant what he said. Sometimes the Gospels make it clear that he cared about the people involved, and felt sorry for them. He wanted to show God's power and that God's kingdom had come.

There are 35 stories in the Gospels which tell of Jesus working miracles. They can be divided into three main groups:

- healings
- nature miracles
- bringing the dead back to life.

Christians believe God's power can heal people today

Many of the stories occur in more than one Gospel. The largest group is stories about how Jesus healed people who were ill. This section looks at two stories about healing.

Jesus heals a man

Once Jesus was in a town where there was a man who was suffering from a dreaded skin-disease. When he saw Jesus, he threw himself down and begged him, 'Sir, if you want to, you can make me clean!'

Jesus stretched out his hand and touched him. 'I do want to,' he answered. 'Be clean!'

At once the disease left the man. Jesus ordered him, 'Don't tell anyone, but go straight to the priest and let him examine you; then to prove you are cured, offer the sacrifice as Moses ordered.'

But news about Jesus spread more and more widely, and crowds of people came to hear him and be healed from their diseases. Luke 5, 12–15

In those days, leprosy was a disease for which there was no cure. People were very afraid of catching it. Anyone who was thought to be suffering from leprosy was forbidden to go anywhere near other people. They had to stay away from towns and villages, even their homes, and shout a warning to make sure that no one came near. Jesus did what no one would have expected – he touched the man. Then he told him to go to the **priest**, because, according to the Jewish law, only a priest could say that the leprosy had been cured.

Jesus heals a blind beggar

As Jesus was coming near Jericho, there was a blind man sitting by the side of the road, begging. When he heard the crowd passing by he asked, 'What is this?'
'Jesus of Nazareth is passing by,' they told him.
He cried out, 'Jesus! Son of David! Take pity on me!'
The people in front scolded him and told him to be quiet. But he shouted even more loudly, 'Son of David! Take pity on me!'
So Jesus stopped and ordered the man to be brought to him. When he came near, Jesus asked him, 'What do you want me to do for you?'
'Sir,' he answered, 'I want to see again.'
Jesus said to him, 'Then see! Your faith has made you well.'
At once he was able to see, and he followed Jesus, giving thanks to God.
Luke 18, 35–43

There are several stories in the Gospels about how Jesus healed people who were blind. This may be because in those days blindness was a common problem. It may also be because the Gospel writers saw these miracles as having a meaning – as **symbols**. Jesus told the people that their faith had cured them. The Gospel writers believed that Jesus gave sight to blind people if they believed he could help them. In the same way, the writers wanted to show that believing in Jesus as the Son of God could bring light to the lives of people who had been 'spiritually blind'.

This story is the only time in the Gospels that anyone calls Jesus 'Son of David'. This was a title that people expected the Messiah to use. For the blind man to use it like this shows that by this stage of his ministry, many people were expecting Jesus to show that he was the Messiah.

Summing up

The stories of miracles that Jesus worked show the way he felt about people, and the way in which the Gospel writers felt about Jesus.

Activities

A

1 Why are there so many miracle stories in the Gospels?

2 In the story of the blind man, why do you think the crowd scolded the man and told him to be quiet? Why do you think he did not do as he was told?

B

3 How many reasons can you think of why Jesus might have told the leper not to tell anyone how he had been cured?

4 Why might the Gospel writers have thought it was especially important to include stories about Jesus healing blindness?

5 Think of five things today that people describe as miracles. Do you think they really are miraculous?

C

6 Find out more about why the title 'Son of David' was so important. (Use books with information about Jewish kings to help you.)

13 Outline of Church history

The First Christians

When Christianity first began, all the followers of Jesus were Jews. They probably had no idea of starting a new religion. They were called Followers of the Way, because they lived in the way that Jesus had taught. They were like several other groups in Judaism who continued to be Jews even though they had a particular belief that other Jews did not share.

But gradually problems began. The followers of Jesus had to work out who could belong to their group. For example, non-Jews heard about the teachings and wanted to become followers of Jesus, too. Was it possible for non-Jews to become followers of Jesus without becoming Jews first? When the Followers decided that it was not necessary for everyone to become a Jew before they became a Christian, the way was open for Christianity to spread much more widely. The break with Judaism had to happen.

Then other problems developed. The Followers did not begin with a complete set of beliefs. They had to work things out gradually. As their beliefs about Jesus became clearer, it became obvious that what they believed about Jesus could not fit with what they had believed as Jews. How could Jesus be the Son of God, when they were sure that there was only one God? As time went on, Christians began to be **persecuted** by the Romans. This means they were punished for what they believed. The persecution was supposed to crush the new religion, but it actually made it stronger because its beliefs became clearer. Christianity became an accepted religion in the Roman Empire in 312 CE, and soon afterwards the Council of Nicaea (325 CE) made the first creed.

How Christianity developed

As the new Church's beliefs became more organized, people began to disagree about them. Gradually, it became clear that opinions were dividing into two. One group was based around the Church in Constantinople. The other was based around the Church in Rome. Disagreements between the two increased, and arguments became more and more bitter. At last, in 1054, the leader in Constantinople refused to accept the authority of the leader in Rome, the **Pope**. The Pope's answer was to declare that the Constantinople group was no longer part of the Church. The split had become complete. The Western group, based in Rome under the leadership of Popes, became the Roman Catholic Church (see pages 30–1)
The Eastern group, based in Constantinople under the leadership of **patriarchs**, became the Orthodox Church (see pages 32–3). Both claimed to be the 'true' Church.

Many early Christians were killed in the Colosseum in Rome

Constantinople is now called Istanbul

The Protestant Churches

In the West, the Roman Catholic Church was the only Church for about 500 years. It was very powerful. Then in the sixteenth century people began to protest about things that they felt were wrong in the way it was run. For example, the Popes, the leaders of the Church, seemed to be more interested in keeping power and living a good life than they were in teaching people about being Christians. The Church became very interested in raising money. Taxes were taken from people who were very poor. If people paid enough money to the Church, they could be given a certificate to say that God had forgiven all the things they had done wrong!

People who felt that things like this were not right split away from the Roman Catholic Church. They began worshipping on their own, and developing beliefs that were slightly different from those of the Roman Catholic Church. Because they had 'protested' about the things that were wrong, they became known as **Protestants**. In the years since that time, many Protestant Churches have developed. New Churches began as people felt there was something wrong with what their Church was teaching, and split away to worship on their own. Sometimes groups have joined together to make new Churches. The different branches of the Church are called **denominations**.

Summing up

Christianity has developed all through its history. Today, all Churches share the main beliefs of Christianity, but they worship in different ways and often have slightly different beliefs.

Activities

A

1 What were the first Christians called? Why were they given this name?

2 How did Protestants get their name?

B

3 Why was it important when the first Christians decided that new followers did not have to become Jews first? What do you think would have happened if they had decided everyone had to become a Jew first?

4 Why do you think that both the Eastern and Western Churches claimed to be the 'true' church when they split apart in 1054?

5 What sort of things did the Protestants feel was wrong with the Roman Catholic Church when they began their protests? Explain why they protested.

C

6 Many people are still persecuted today for what they believe. Think of as many examples as you can of people in the twentieth century who have been persecuted. List as many reasons as you can why people refuse to give up what they believe, even when they are being punished for it.

14 The Roman Catholic

The Roman Catholic Church is the oldest group in Western Christianity. It is also the largest. In 1994 about 900 million people were Roman Catholic – about half of all Christians in the world. In 1995 there were over 5 million Roman Catholics in the UK, with 4348 churches.

The Pope

The Pope is the head of the Church. Roman Catholics believe that the authority of the Popes comes from the Apostles, especially St Peter. The word 'pope' comes from a Latin word which means father, so the Pope is like a father to the Church. Popes have a special authority. A Pope is elected by the most senior men in the Church who are called **cardinals**. Once chosen, he remains Pope until he dies.

Priests

A priest is a man who has been **ordained**. Ordained really means 'set apart'. It means the priests have been blessed at a special service. They have been specially trained to lead worship and to help ordinary people to live as Christians.

An open-air Mass led by Pope John Paul II

Lighting candles is part of worship

Roman Catholics believe that priests are the link between ordinary people and God. Women are not allowed to become priests, and priests are not allowed to marry, so that they are free to concentrate on their work. **Bishops** are senior priests. They are responsible for running the Church, and for ordaining priests to work in local churches. Senior bishops are called **archbishops**. The titles priest, bishop and archbishop are used by other churches as well as the Roman Catholic Church.

Saints

One of the ways in which Roman Catholic beliefs are different from those of other Western Christians is the place they give to **saints**. A saint is someone who was especially close to God when they were alive. Many Christians believe that this means saints are still special after death. Roman Catholics often pray to saints, because they believe that this makes it more likely that God will answer the prayer. Their churches usually have statues of the saints. People do not worship the statues, but Roman Catholics believe that the statues help them worship God, because they help them to concentrate.

The Virgin Mary

Roman Catholics believe that Mary is very important because she was the mother of Jesus when he was alive on earth. They do not worship her because she is not God, but they often pray to her. One of the most popular prayers is called the **Angelus**, or Ave Maria.

Hail, Mary, full of grace,
The Lord is with thee,
Blessed art thou among women,
and blessed is the fruit of thy womb Jesus.
Holy Mary, mother of God,
pray for us sinners, now, and at the hour of our death.

Confession

Because Roman Catholics believe that the priest is the link between the people and God, they think that it is important for people to go to the priest to confess the things they have done wrong. Years ago, **Confession** was usually held in a small room with a screen in the middle, so that the priest could not see who he was talking to. Today, this is not usually thought to be necessary. When the person has confessed everything they have done wrong, the priest can tell them what to do to show that they are really sorry. Then he can 'speak for' God and tell them that their sins have been forgiven. Roman Catholics are usually expected to go to Confession at least once a year. A priest must never tell anyone what he has been told in Confession.

Confession

Mass

The most important Roman Catholic service is called **Mass**. Most of the words for Mass are written in a special service book called a **Missal**. There are many different types of Mass. Mass always includes the service called the Eucharist or Holy Communion. This is the service when Christians remember the last meal that Jesus ate with his disciples.

Summing up

The Roman Catholic Church is the oldest and largest branch of Western Christianity.

Activities

A

1. About how many people in the world are Christians?
2. What are saints? Why do Roman Catholics pray to them?

B

3. Look up Matthew 16, 18–19. What does this tell you about why Roman Catholics believe the authority of the Popes comes from St Peter?
4. Why are priests so important for Roman Catholics?
5. What does the Angelus prayer tell you about what how Roman Catholics think of the Virgin Mary?

C

6. How do you think Roman Catholics feel after they have been to Confession? Why do you think they find Confession helpful? What do you think are the advantages and disadvantages of being expected to tell someone else the things you have done wrong?

15 The Orthodox Churches

The Orthodox Churches form the second largest group in Christianity. Most Orthodox Christians today live in eastern Europe or Russia, though there are many thousands of Orthodox Christians living in western countries. About half a million Orthodox Christians live in the UK. The two main groups of Orthodox Christians are Greek Orthodox and Russian Orthodox.

Orthodox is a Greek word which means 'right praise or worship'. Orthodox Christians believe that they continue the Church as Jesus began it. Many of the beliefs of the Orthodox Churches are the same as those of other Christians, but there are important differences.

Orthodox churches

Orthodox churches are usually square or sometimes in the shape of a cross. They are divided into two parts (sometimes three) by screens. The main screen is called an **iconostasis**. It divides the **nave**, the main part of the church, from the **sanctuary**, which is the holiest part of the church. The nave does not usually contain seats, except for a few round the walls for elderly or disabled people. Orthodox Christians stand to worship. This is because standing upright is something that makes human beings different from animals. There are no musical instruments in an Orthodox church because although all Orthodox services are sung, the singing is always unaccompanied.

Icons

Icons are an important part of worship for Orthodox Christians. An icon is a picture of Jesus, the Virgin Mary or one of the saints. Icons are painted very carefully, and the painting follows strict rules, so that every icon of a particular person will look more or less the same. Orthodox Christians do not worship the icons, but they stand in front of them to pray because they believe this helps to give their prayers a focus and helps them concentrate.

The iconostasis

The iconostasis is the screen that divides the nave from the sanctuary. Iconostasis means 'place where icons are put', and the screen always has several icons on it. It has doors, in the centre. There is always an icon of Jesus on the right of the doors and one of the Virgin Mary on the left. The iconostasis hides the **altar** from the rest of the church. The altar is the table that is used for the service of Holy Communion. Orthodox Christians call this service the **Liturgy**. Only the priest goes through the doors in the iconostasis, but they are opened at certain times during the Liturgy. This is to show that through Jesus it is possible to reach God.

An Orthodox church in Birmingham (notice the inconostasis)

Lighting a candle in front of an icon is part of worship

Priests

Services in an Orthodox church are led by a priest or a bishop. There are two groups of priests in Orthodox churches. Some priests are **monks**, men who have made special promises to dedicate their lives to God. One of the promises that they make is that they will not marry. Bishops are chosen from the monks. A priest who looks after the people in a local church is expected to be married.

The Liturgy

The Liturgy is the name that Orthodox Christians give to the service of Holy Communion. The Liturgy used most often is called the Liturgy of St John Chrysostom, who was an important Church leader in the fourth century CE. The Liturgy is divided into three parts. In the first part, the priest prepares the bread and wine. In the second part, he comes into the nave and swings a special container of burning **incense** (sweet smelling spices) in front of the icons and the people. A copy of the Gospels is carried in procession through the church. Hymns are sung, and there are prayers and readings from the Bible. The third part of the service, when people are given the bread and wine, is the most serious. All Orthodox Christians are allowed to take part in this, but adults are expected to prepare for it carefully. They should **fast** beforehand and they are usually expected to have been to Confession, too.

Summing up

Orthodox Christians live mainly in eastern Europe and Russia. The Orthodox Churches are an important branch of Christianity.

Activities

A

1. What is an iconostasis? Explain why the doors are so important.
2. Why do Orthodox Churches not usually contain chairs?

B

3. Icons are very important to Orthodox Christians. Explain what an icon is, and why focussing attention on it may help an Orthodox Christian to worship.
4. Using their hand to make the sign of the cross, kissing icons and smelling incense are some of the ways Orthodox Christians worship. Why do you think they believe it is so important that their whole body is involved in their worship?
5. Why do you think that Orthodox Christians fast before they receive the bread and wine at Communion?

C

6. How many reasons can you give why the Orthodox Churches teach that priests who look after local churches should be married, but senior priests should not be?

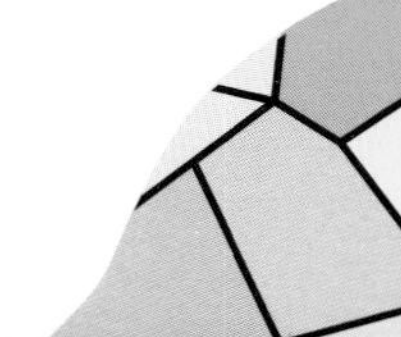

16 The Anglican Churches

There are Anglican Churches all over the world. In the UK, the Anglican Churches are the Church of England, the Episcopal Church in Scotland, the Church in Wales and the Church of Ireland. In America it is called the Episcopal Church of the USA. In other countries, it usually takes its name from the country, for example the Anglican Church of Australia. All Anglican Churches respect the Church of England as their mother Church, but they are not governed by it.

The Church of England is 'Established'. In other words, it is the official Church in England. This means it has a special part to play in the way the country is governed. This is why the Queen is the head of the Church. It is also the reason why Church of England bishops have the right to sit in the House of Lords.

Anglican clergy

Clergy is a word which means anyone who has been ordained in any of the Christian Churches.

Morning worship in an Anglican church in Bristol

Anglican archbishops from all over the world meeting in London

In Anglican Churches, the most important clergy are bishops. (The Latin word *episcopus* means bishop, and this is why some Anglican Churches are called Episcopal.) Senior bishops are called archbishops. In the Church of England, the most important is the Archbishop of Canterbury. Clergy who look after a local area may have any one of several different titles. Most are called **vicars** or **rectors**. There used to be a difference between these two, but today they are usually the same. Most Anglican Churches now allow women to become vicars.

Anglican churches

A **cathedral** is a bishop's church. It takes its name from the **cathedra** – the bishop's throne – which it contains. This is the only reason for it being a cathedral. Many cathedrals are very old and beautifully decorated. Local churches are often called **parish** churches because Anglicans call the local area a parish. Most parish churches are dedicated to a saint (for example, the parish church of St Peter).

Worship

Worship in Anglican Churches is based on a Service Book in which the 'pattern' for a service is written down. In the Church of England, this used to be called the Prayer Book. The modern version is called the Alternative Service Book.

Anglican Churches celebrate the service of Holy Communion at least once every week. Sometimes it is a special service early on a Sunday morning. At other times, there is a Family Communion, which is held during the main service. Holy Communion services are also held on special days in the year. Services in an Anglican Church often have special names. The first service in a morning is called Matins. The service in an evening is called Evensong.

When someone goes to a service in an Anglican Church, they usually bow their head towards the altar as they first sit down. They may kneel to pray before the service begins. The service contains hymns, readings from the Bible and prayers. Sometimes **psalms** are said or sung. The psalms are 150 special poems in the Bible. There is also often a talk by the vicar or person leading the service. This is called a **sermon**. It is usually based on a teaching in the Bible. The vicar explains the teaching and uses the sermon to teach the people more about what being a Christian means. There is usually an organ or other musical instruments to lead the singing, and in most churches there is a choir. The people usually join in singing hymns, but they may listen to the choir singing during the worship, too.

Although this describes typical Anglican worship, it is important to notice that not all Anglican Churches worship in the same way. Some congregations prefer worship that is quite like the worship in Roman Catholic Churches. Others worship in ways that are less formal, and more like Free Church or Evangelical worship. It really depends on what the vicar and the people are comfortable with.

Summing up

The Anglican Churches are important members of the worldwide Christian Church.

Activities

A

1. Why are some Anglican Churches called Episcopal?
2. What makes a church a cathedral?

B

3. Imagine that you have attended an Anglican service one Sunday morning. Write an account of what you saw and heard.
4. Use a Bible to find out the words of at least one psalm. Why do you think Christians find it helpful to use psalms that were written thousands of years ago in their worship?
5. The Church of England decided in 1992 to allow women to become vicars. The subject still causes a lot of discussion and disagreement. Why do you think people have such strong views about it? What is your opinion?

C

6. A sermon uses Bible stories to teach people about living as Christians. Look back at unit 11 (pages 24–5). Choose one of the parables mentioned there, and discuss with a partner what sort of things might be included in a sermon based on it. Write down what you decide.

17 Other Protestant Churches

Protestant Churches in the UK that are not Anglican are called the Free Churches. This includes groups such as the Presbyterian, Methodist and Baptist Churches. They are called 'Free' because they are not Established like the Church of England. This was very important when these Churches were being formed.

All the Free Churches are similar in some ways. Their services are usually less formal, and they do not always use service books. In most Free Churches, women can be ordained, and most of the Churches encourage members who are not ordained to take part in, or lead, services. Each of the Free Churches has details of belief and ways of worship that are different from all the other Churches.

Presbyterian Churches

The Presbyterian Churches form the largest group of Free Churches in the UK. The main Churches are the Church of Scotland, the Presbyterian Church in Ireland, the Presbyterian Church of Wales and the United Reformed Church. There are also several other smaller branches. The name Presbyterian comes from a Greek word that means **minister**, which is the name they give to their clergy. Presbyterian Churches have this name because they are governed by ministers rather than by bishops.

Methodist Church

The Methodist Church is the second biggest Free Church in the UK. In 1995 it had 1.3 million members. It was begun by a man called John Wesley in the eighteenth century. He spent most of his life preaching to people, travelling thousands of kilometres on horseback around Britain, Ireland and America. The name Methodist comes from the 'method' that John Wesley encouraged people to use in their lives.

A Methodist service

Baptist Church

The Baptist Church got its name because it does not baptize babies. Baptists believe that someone who is being baptized should be old enough to understand why the service is so important, so baptisms in the Baptist Church are usually held for people who are in their teens or older. Like some other Churches, Baptists baptize by **total immersion** (see page 54).

The Salvation Army

The Salvation Army was begun by William Booth in the nineteenth century. He believed that it was important to look after the conditions in which people lived, as well as think about what they believed. He called the movement he began an army because he thought that being a Christian was like being a soldier fighting against evil. Members of the Salvation Army wear uniforms, and have the same titles as soldiers. The head of the Salvation Army is called the General. Today, many members of the Salvation Army work with people who are homeless, or addicted to alcohol or drugs.

The Society of Friends

The Society of Friends was begun by a man called George Fox in the sixteenth century. Members of the Society are often called 'Quakers'. This is because the early members were often seen to tremble with emotion, and the nickname they were given then stuck. Friends do not have clergy, and their worship is very simple. They sit quietly until one of the group feels that God has given him or her something to say. They believe that this time of quiet in a busy, noisy world helps them to become better Christians. All Friends are pacifists, which means they do not believe in fighting. They believe that disagreements, whether between individuals or between countries, should be solved peacefully and without violence.

Evangelical and Pentecostal Churches

There are some groups of Pentecostal Churches – for example, the Assemblies of God. Many other Pentecostal and Evangelical Churches are independent or part of a very small group. Their worship may be very lively with clapping and dancing, although some Churches do not agree with this. Evangelical and Pentecostal Churches tend to concentrate in their worship on the work of the Holy Spirit. Members are expected to show how the Holy Spirit works in their lives.

Many Free Churches have women ministers

Summing up

Different Churches are organized in different ways. Even small differences may be very important for the people who worship there, because their religion is so important in their lives.

Activities

A

1 Why are the Churches described in this unit called 'Free'?

2 What happens in a meeting of the Society of Friends? Why do Friends find this sort of worship helpful?

B

3 John Wesley said, 'The world is my parish'. What do you think he meant? How does this help to explain the way he spent his life?

4 What does pacifism mean? Why do you think many Christians feel that it is part of their religion to be a pacifist?

5 Members of the Salvation Army spend a lot of time working with people who are poor or homeless. Explain why they feel that this is an important part of being a Christian. (Looking up Matthew 25, 37–40 may help you to answer this.)

C

6 Find out more about one of the Churches mentioned in this unit. Work in groups of three or four on a project about when and how the Church began, and what it is like today.

18 Christian worship

Be still, for the presence of the Lord,
the Holy One is here.
Come, bow before him now, with
reverence and fear.
In him no sin is found, we stand on
holy ground,
Be still for the presence of the Lord,
the Holy One is here.

Be still for the power of the Lord is
moving in this place,
He comes to cleanse and heal,
to minister his grace.
No work too hard for him, in faith
receive from him;
Be still, for the power of the Lord is
moving in this place.

by D. J. Evans

This is part of a modern hymn which sums up many of the things that Christians believe about worshipping God. The word worship comes from an Old English word which means 'give worth to' – in other words, to show how much you value something. Christians believe that worshipping God both alone and in a group is an important part of their lives.

When do Christians worship?

Christians believe that they can worship God anywhere and at any time. They may want to worship because they are looking at a beautiful painting or a lovely view, or listening to a piece of music. They may feel that they can worship by helping other people. As well as individual experiences like this, most Christians feel that meeting as a group to worship is important. A meeting for worship is usually called a service. Sometimes services are held out of doors, but more often they are held in a church.

Church services can be held on any day of the week, but regular services take place on a Sunday because that is the day on which Christians believe Jesus rose from the dead.

Church worship

Different groups of Christians worship in different ways. In some Churches, worship is a time for being quiet and thoughtful, as the hymn at the start of this unit suggests. In other Churches, worship includes dancing and clapping with people joining in by shouting things like 'Praise the Lord' and 'Hallelujah!'. What one Christian finds helpful in worship may make another feel very uncomfortable. The different styles of worship in different denominations mean that Christians can choose to worship in a way that they find suits them best. Whether the worship is quiet or lively, there are some things that are included in almost all services.

- Singing, either with a choir leading the worship or with the people joining in hymns.
- Praising God. This means thanking him for everything that he has done in their lives and especially for giving his son Jesus to the world. People may praise God by singing hymns or songs, or by saying prayers.

Most services are held in a church

Prayer and praise are part of worship

- Prayer – talking and listening to God. As well as praise, prayers may be a time for thinking about people who are in trouble or who need special prayers for some reason.
- Bible readings.
- A sermon, which is a talk by the priest or person leading the service. It may explain part of the Bible, or be about something that affects the lives of the people listening.
- A talk for children, or something that involves particular groups in the church.

Group worship

Some Christian meetings are held every year where large groups of Christians from different Churches and backgrounds can meet and share their faith. One of several events in Britain is a Christian pop festival called *Greenbelt*. This is held every August Bank Holiday, when many thousands of Christians go to camp for the weekend. They share in music concerts, listening to pop stars who are Christians, as well as taking part in huge open-air services.

Other ways of worshipping

Many Christians believe that they can worship in other ways. Feeling the power of God through nature or art is one way of worshipping.

Some Christians feel that they can worship by caring for other people. They may work with people who are homeless or addicted to drugs, or help to look after people who are disabled. Their care comes from the belief that God loves everyone and it is part of their duty as a Christian to show this love for other people.

Summing up

Worship means praising God and asking for his help. Worship is important for Christians because it gives them a chance to feel close to God.

Activities

A

1. What does worship mean?
2. Why do some Christians believe that it is important to help people who are not as fortunate as themselves?

B

3. What are the different ways in which Christians can worship? Explain why not all Christians want to worship in the same way.
4. Why do you think people who believe in God might want to worship him when they are looking at something beautiful?
5. What are the parts of church worship that are found in almost all denominations? Why do you think that Christians feel these things are most important?

C

6. Write a hymn or a prayer which shows how a Christian might praise God.

19 Different ways of worship

This unit was written by two Christians who worship in very different ways. Lalini is a Roman Catholic. Angelika attends an Evangelical Church in Chester.

A Roman Catholic Family Mass

'A family Mass is usually on Sunday morning. As the priest goes to the altar, we sing an entrance hymn. There are usually another four or five hymns during the service. The priest and the congregation exchange greetings. If there is a Children's Liturgy Group in the church, the children who are between three and eleven years old will usually leave the service at this point. They have their own readings and activities while the Mass is going on.

'We think about the ways we have failed to be the loving people that God wants us to be, and we tell God and each other that we are sorry. On Sundays there are three readings from the Bible. The most important one is from the Gospels. During the homily (sermon) the priest explains the readings we have just heard, and how they relate to our daily lives.

Lalini with Ruth and Steve outside their church

'After more prayers, the children rejoin the congregation. They form a procession and bring the bread and wine to the priest for the Communion. We give praise and thanks to God, then join in saying the Lord's Prayer. We exchange a sign of peace by shaking hands with those people around us. We pray silently for a while, then we go up to the altar to receive the Communion. The priest blesses us in the name of Jesus. It is time for us to leave in peace to love and serve the Lord in our actions.

'I feel that a Catholic Mass is the right way of worship for me because there is a set order of service during which we have the opportunity to worship together, as well as to think about things on our own. I know that I can communicate with God anywhere, but in this busy world it helps to have a special time set aside for prayer and praise. It also gives me a sense of fellowship with others of the same faith. Wherever I am in the world, I can walk into a Roman Catholic church and be able to follow the Mass. This is because it will be celebrated in almost the same way as in my own church, even if it is in another language.'

A typical evangelical service

'As you go into an evangelical service, you may find a traditional church building with pews, but you are more likely to find a modern building with chairs. The person leading the service, called the minister, would not be wearing robes but normal clothes. There would not be an organ but a band with drums, keyboards, guitars, and maybe a sax or a flute and singers.

'The service starts. The band plays modern worship songs, some quiet and worshipful, others bouncy and lively. People join in and sing. Depending on what the songs express, people sit down quietly or stand with hands raised to God, or they may clap and dance with joy.

Angelika

'In the breaks between the songs, people say prayers of thanks and praise to God. Someone may read a passage from the Bible that he or she feels is important to share with other people. Or there may be someone giving a prophecy, which is a message from God to encourage or direct people in the church. Although the worship is led by the minister, it depends very much on how people join in and respond to God. After the worship, the children and teenagers leave for their Bible classes while the adults stay to listen to the preacher. He talks about part of the Bible, or something else important for the life of a Christian.

'Some Christians prefer this lively style of worship. The Bible says that we should love God with all our heart, all our soul, and all our strength. It also tells us how people used to praise God by singing songs, making music, raising their hands, clapping and dancing. We believe that when you allow Jesus to be part of your life and change you, you experience God's love and help in your everyday life. This lively worship style expresses how excited people are about who God is and what he has done for them. Would you be sitting down quietly if you were at a really exciting football match?'

Summing up

Different ways of worship are important, so that all Christians can worship in a way with which they feel comfortable.

Activities

A

1. Find at least five ways in which the services in the two Churches differ from each other.
2. Find at least five ways in which services in the two Churches are the same.

B

3. What part of a Roman Catholic Mass do you think is the most important?
4. Why do you think it is the children who take the bread and wine to the priest in the Roman Catholic service?
5. What reasons does Angelika give for why Christians at an evangelical service enjoy the lively worship? Can you think of any other reasons why some people might prefer this sort of worship?

C

6. Write a description in your own words of what happens in these two types of services. Then say which sort of worship you think you would prefer, and why.

20 Signs and symbols used in worship

Signs and symbols are very important in Christianity. A symbol is usually a picture or image that stands for something. Symbols are often used as a way of explaining things that would be very complicated to put into words. Signs are used for Christianity itself, and to show different things that happen in the life of the Church.

Signs for Christianity

The sign most often used today for Christianity is a cross. This is because Jesus was crucified. Sometimes a cross with a figure of Jesus on it is used instead. This is called a **crucifix**. However, in the early days of Christianity it was not common for people to use this sign. It was so horrible and shameful that no one wanted to use it. Probably the nearest we can imagine is that it would have been like someone today using a picture of a gallows or an electric chair as symbols to show their religion.

Different shapes of crosses

There are many different shapes of crosses. The † shaped one we usually think of is called a Latin cross. One with three steps at the bottom is called a calvary cross, and some crosses are made in the shape of an anchor. A Maltese cross is a black cross with eight points on a white background. It gets its name from the Middle Ages, when it was used by the Knights of Malta.

In the early days of Christianity, the most common sign used by Christians was the sign of a fish. There were two reasons for this. One is that many of the early disciples were fishermen, and Jesus had told them that he would make them 'fishers of men'. The other is because of what the sign could stand for. In the Greek language, the word for fish is *ichthus*. If each letter is made into the first letter of a Greek word, *ichthus* begins the words which mean 'Jesus Christ, God's Son, Saviour'. So a fish can be used as a symbol for the most important things that Christians believe.

Alpha and omega (Α and Ω)

Alpha and omega are the first and last letters of the Greek alphabet. They are often used in Christianity as a symbol for Jesus. This is because Christians believe that Jesus was the beginning and the end – in other words, the most important person who has ever lived.

The four Gospels

Each of the four Gospel writers has a symbol which is used for him. St Matthew's symbol is the figure of a man. St Mark's symbol is a lion, St Luke's is an ox. St John's is an eagle. Although St Peter did not write a Gospel, his symbol is quite often found in churches, too.

It is a pair of keys, one crossed over the other. This is because the Bible says that Jesus told Peter, 'I will give you the keys of the kingdom of heaven' (Matthew 16, 18).

Colours

Colours are often used as symbols in worship. In some churches the altar has a cloth cover. The priest or vicar may wear a special scarf over his other robes, too. The colours of these cloths change according to what time of year it is. The Church year is divided into 'seasons', just like an ordinary year. The first season is Advent, followed by Christmas, Epiphany, Lent and Easter. After Pentecost and Trinity Sunday, the remaining time – almost half the year – is 'weeks after Trinity'.

Purple is a symbol for penitence – being sorry for the things that you have done wrong. This is the colour that is used for Advent and Lent, both of which are serious times for Christians. White or gold is used for the most important festivals of Christmas and Easter, and at Epiphany. Pentecost is red, because red is like fire. Christians believe Pentecost is the time when God gave the disciples the Holy Spirit, and the Bible says it came like fire. Green is the colour for nature, so it is a symbol for growth. It is used between the special times in the calendar.

Red is the colour used at Pentecost

Summing up

Many symbols are used in worship, because Christians find that they help to make important things clear to the people worshipping.

Activities

A

1. What is a symbol? Why do Christians use symbols in their worship?
2. What colours are used during the Church year? Explain what each of the colours stands for.

B

3. Why did the early Christians not want to use the sign of the cross? Why do you think Christians today are much more ready to use it?
4. Explain why the early Christians used the shape of a fish as a symbol for their religion.
5. The crossed keys of St Peter are a symbol of the keys of the kingdom of heaven. What sort of symbols would you use to describe heaven? (Remember that 'picture language' can be a sort of symbol.)

C

6. Find out more about one set of symbols mentioned in this unit. Work in pairs or small groups to put together a wall display showing what you have found out, with drawings to illustrate it.

21 *Church buildings – outside*

A church is the place where Christians go to worship. Some churches are among the oldest and most beautiful buildings in the world. Other churches may be in ordinary houses, or no more than one room in a normal house. From the beginning of Christianity, some people have argued that Christians do not need a building to worship in – the message of Christianity can be preached in the open air, new Christians can be baptized in a river or other water, and the Eucharist can be celebrated around any table. But like almost all other religions, Christians have always wanted special buildings in which to worship.

Early churches

While Christians were being persecuted in the Roman Empire, special buildings were never used for worship because people known to be Christians would be arrested. It was only after Christianity became an accepted religion that churches began to be built. Then the pattern Christians used was the one from the most important Roman buildings. These were usually built in the shape of a rectangle, divided into three with pillars. The largest area was in the middle, with a higher roof to allow for windows; there were two smaller areas, one at each side. This is still the basic shape for many churches today.

Cathedrals

The most important churches for Orthodox, Roman Catholic and Anglican Christians are called cathedrals. Many cathedrals are very old, and are covered in carvings and decorations. At the time when they were built, ordinary people lived in very poor and simple houses. There was a great difference between these houses and the enormous, beautifully decorated cathedrals. The differences helped to give ordinary people a sense of the importance of worship and religion.

Lincoln cathedral still towers over the buildings around it

Roman Catholic churches

Roman Catholic churches are usually built in the shape of a cross or a rectangle, but those built in recent years may be round or octagonal. They can often be recognized by the fact that they have one or more statues outside. The statues may be of the Virgin Mary, or of Jesus or the saint to whom the church is dedicated.

Orthodox churches

Orthodox churches are usually square, so that all the people worshipping can feel involved in the service. They are often very plain outside, but richly decorated inside. This helps to remind the people of the difference between this life and life after death. A Greek Orthodox church often has a dome as part of the roof. Russian Orthodox churches often have several short towers with domes on the top.

In most western countries, only a few Orthodox churches have been specially built. Most are in buildings that have been changed so that they can be used as churches.

Anglican churches

Most Anglican churches are built in the shape of a cross. They usually have a tower or spire, which reminds people that they should 'look up' to God. Many are hundreds of years old, and the architecture can often tell the church's history. Thick walls and arches usually mean that the church is very old. More graceful pointed windows and arches are usually more recent. A typical Anglican church also has a graveyard around it.

Free Church churches

In England, most Free Church churches were built in the nineteenth century. Some have small spires or towers, but most are very plain and simple outside. Churches of the same denomination often look similar. Much depends on when they were built.

A small Methodist church

Summing up

Having a special place to worship is very important for most Christians. They want the church to look beautiful, to show their love for God.

Activities

A

1 Why did the early Christians not have special places for worship?

2 How might you recognize an Orthodox church?

B

3 Why do you think early churches were in the same style as important Roman buildings?

4 Great cathedrals are often very impressive buildings today. Explain why they looked even more impressive when they were built. Why was this important?

5 Making churches beautiful is one way of showing love for God. How many other ways can you think of in which Christians can show their love for God?

C

6 Most religions have special places for their worship. Why do you think it is important to have a special place for worship? Write a short article about a place that is special for you, saying why you feel it is important.

22 Church buildings – inside

Some churches can be quite different to other churches inside, because denominations worship in different ways. For example, there is a great difference between the worship in an Orthodox church and the worship in an Evangelical house group. So what the two denominations need as 'props' for their worship is quite different, too. This section looks at the things that you are likely to find in most churches.

Altar

The altar is the most important piece of furniture in most churches. It is the table used for the service of the Eucharist. In older churches, an altar is usually made of wood or stone, and is at the east end of the church, opposite the main entrance. It is separated from the rest of the church by a rail and sometimes by steps. It is in the area called the sanctuary. In Orthodox churches, the altar is separated from the main body of the church by the iconostasis. In most Free churches there is a Communion table rather than an altar. It is usually made of wood, and is plain and simple.

Pews, pulpit, altar and lectern in an Anglican church in Essex

Pulpit

The pulpit is an enclosed raised area, usually near the front of a church. It is reached by climbing a short flight of steps. In many Free churches, the pulpit is the most noticeable part, and is used by the preacher for the whole service. In other churches, the pulpit is only used by the person who is giving the sermon, the special talk which is an important part of most services.

Lectern

Many churches have a special reading desk where the Bible is kept. This is called a lectern. It is often made of brass and is in the shape of an eagle, though no one really knows why. The bird's claws usually rest on a ball, which represents the world. Some people think that resting the Bible on the eagle's wings is a symbol showing Christianity being carried all over the world.

Font

Churches which baptize people need a place to put the water that is used for baptism. This special bowl is called the **font**. The bowl is placed in a carved stand, usually made of wood or stone. In Anglican churches it is near the door – a way of showing that baptism is entry to the Church. In most Free churches it is near the Communion table – a way of showing that the Eucharist and baptism are closely connected.

Some Churches baptize by total immersion, when the person's whole body is immersed under the water (this is explained on pages 54–5). A font would not be large enough for this type of baptism, so these churches usually have part of the floor that can be used as a pool.

Seats

Most modern churches have ordinary chairs for people to sit on, but older churches usually have special benches which are called pews. In an Orthodox church, where the congregation normally stands for worship, the only seats are likely to be around the walls of the church.

Decorations

Many different sorts of decoration are used in churches. In Orthodox churches, the icons are very important. In Roman Catholic churches, there are usually statues around the walls. Candles and lamps are used in many churches. Many people think this is to represent Jesus as the Light of the World, one of the names that Christians use for him. All these things are to help people worship. Banners decorate the church, and can be used when members take part in activities outside the church, to show which church they come from. Stained glass in the windows helps to make the church beautiful and can also tell stories from the Bible.

A modern stained glass window

Summing up

A church is a place for Christian worship. Some of the things found inside are there because they are necessary; others are to make the building look attractive.

Activities

A

1 Describe three of the most important things you are likely to find in most churches. What is each used for?

2 Which denomination's churches do you think are likely to have the most decorations?

B

3 No one really knows why a lectern is often in the shape of an eagle. Think of some reasons why this bird might be a good symbol for Christianity.

4 Why do you think Christians call Jesus the 'Light of the World'? How can candles be a symbol of this?

5 Why should the decorations in a church help people to worship?

C

6 This and the previous unit have been about special buildings for worship. If you were designing a new church building, how would you show that it was special? Decide which denomination you would like your church to be, then sketch the outside and do a plan for the inside. Other units in this section may help you.

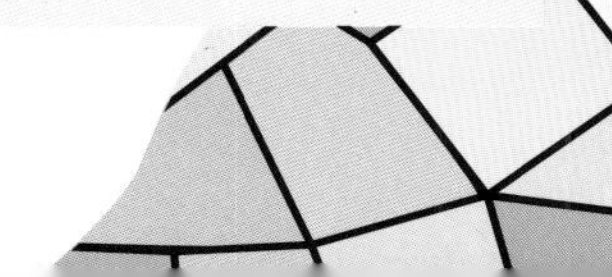

23 History of the Bible

Lord thy word abideth,
And our footsteps guideth,
Who its truth believeth,
Light and joy receiveth.

O that we, discerning
Its most holy learning,
Lord, may love and fear thee,
Ever more be near thee.

Henry William Baker (1821–77)

This is part of an old hymn, which describes how important the Bible is. The language is probably quite different from the way most people today would describe how they feel about it, but it sums up the importance of the Bible for many Christians.

What is the Bible?

The Bible is the Christian holy book. It is made up of two parts, the Old **Testament** and the New Testament. Testament comes from a word that means 'agreement'. Christians believe they are about agreements between God and human beings. Both the Old and New Testaments are collections of books that have been put together. There are 39 books in the Old Testament, and 27 in the New Testament, making 66 books altogether.

The Bible has sold more copies all over the world than any other book. It has been more widely distributed than any other book, too. At the end of 1995 at least a part of the Bible had been translated into 2123 different languages or dialects. As well as being used by Christians as their holy book, stories from the Bible have inspired poets, artists and writers for nearly 2000 years.

Outline history of the Bible

Most of the books of the Old Testament come from the Jewish Scriptures. They were written down over several hundred years, so long ago that no one really knows when. We know that the first five books of the Old Testament had already been put together by the fifth century BCE. The rest of the Jewish Scriptures (24 books altogether) were organized by the second century BCE.

The books of the New Testament were written down in Greek during the first century CE, but it was another 100 years before they were put together in an organized way. The final form of the New Testament was settled after meetings of Church leaders in 367 CE for the Eastern Church, and 393 CE in the Western Church.

The Bible in English

The first translation of the Bible into English was begun in the seventh century. One of the earliest surviving manuscripts is called the Lindisfarne Gospels. This was first written in Latin in about 700 CE, but an English translation was added about 200 years later. In the Middle Ages, a preacher called John Wycliffe translated the Bible into English because he felt that ordinary people ought to be able to read it for themselves more easily. This translation was very important.

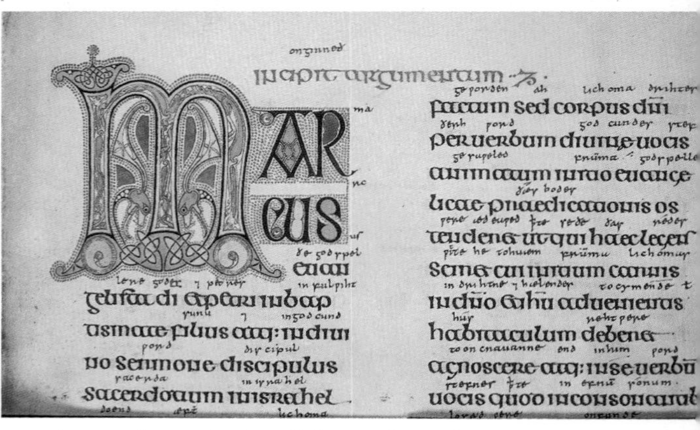

A page from the Lindisfarne Gospels

The medieval chained library in Hereford Catheral

In the Middle Ages, all books had to be written out by hand. Bibles were usually written by monks, and were often beautifully decorated. They were rare and very expensive. The invention of printing made a huge difference to the number of books that were available, and to their cost. The first New Testament to be printed in English was published in 1525, translated from Greek by a man called William Tyndale. Over the next 100 years, several other versions of the Bible were produced. The most important was the King James' version. This was first printed in 1611, and got its name from the fact that King James I ordered it to be done. This translation is still used by many Christians today. The language is old-fashioned, but many people feel that it has a beauty which makes up for the fact that today it is not always easy to understand.

Many other English translations of the Bible have been made in the last 100 years. One of the most popular is the *Good News Bible*, which was published in 1976. This is the translation from which all the Biblical quotations in this book are taken.

Summing up

Because they believe the Bible is so important, Christians have always made great efforts to be able to read it.

Activities

A

1. Explain why the invention of printing made such a difference to the number of Bibles that were available.
2. Why is the King James' version of the Bible still popular 400 years after it was made?

B

3. Why do you think meetings of Church leaders were necessary before the contents of the Bible could be agreed?
4. Many of the poets and artists who have been inspired by the Bible have not been Christians. How many reasons can you think of why they might have used Bible stories?
5. Some religions teach that their holy books should not be translated out of the language in which they were written. The Bible has been translated into over 2000 languages. What are the advantages and disadvantages of translating such an important book?

C

6. Imagine you are a Christian who has just been given a copy of the Bible written in your own language. It is the first time you have been able to read it for yourself. Write a short article saying how you feel.

24 What's in the Bible?

The first part of the Bible, the Old Testament, is the same as some of the Jewish holy books. Jesus was a Jew, and so were all the early Christians, and some of the beliefs of Christians and Jews are very similar. The New Testament is the story of Jesus and of the early years of Christianity. It contains important Christian writings.

The word Testament really means the same as **'Covenant'**. A Covenant is a serious agreement. Jews believe that they have a Covenant with God, which is written down in the books of Genesis and Exodus. Christians believe that Jesus overturned this agreement, and made a new Covenant, in which his death means that people who believe in him can gain a new life with God. This is why Christians call the two sets of the books the Old and New Testaments.

The Old Testament

There are four main groups of books in the Old Testament. It begins with the five books of teaching: Genesis, Exodus, Leviticus, Numbers and Deuteronomy. These books tell of the beginning of the world and of the early days of Judaism. Then there are history books, which describe how the Jews developed as a nation. The third section, poetry books, are mainly poems in praise of God. The most well-used book in this group is the Book of Psalms. Psalms are often used in Christian worship. The largest group of books in the Old Testament are books of the **prophets**. The prophets were messengers from God. They taught the Jews about what God wanted from them.

The Old Testament shows how the Jews gradually learned more about what God is like. Christians believe that it looks forward to the coming of Jesus as God's Messiah. Jews do not believe this because they do not accept that Jesus was the Messiah.

The New Testament

The New Testament is the story of the early years of Christianity. It begins with the four Gospels.

The four Gospels

Gospel comes from an old word that means 'good news'. The men who wrote the Gospels wanted to share what they believed was the good news about Jesus. They were not trying to write a complete story of his life. They were writing about why they believed he was the Son of God. This explains why many of the details that we would expect to find in a life story are missing from the Gospels. It also explains why the four Gospels are not exactly the same. Some stories appear in all four Gospels, but each writer chose to include the material that he thought was most important. The first three Gospels (Matthew, Mark and Luke) are quite similar. John's Gospel is written in quite a different style, and most people agree that it was probably written later.

The symbols of the Gospel writers

Reading the Bible is important for Christians

The Acts of the Apostles

The book of Acts was probably written by the same person who wrote Luke's Gospel, and it continues the story of Christianity from the end of the Gospel. Apostles is the word used for the first Christian preachers. Most of them had been friends of Jesus and had listened to him preaching. A lot of the book of Acts is about the journeys that were made by St Paul, who was one of the most important Christian preachers who has ever lived.

Letters

There are 21 letters in the New Testament. Most of them were written by St Paul to groups of friends. He wrote the letters to teach them about how they should live as Christians, and to give them advice. The letters are in the Bible because the advice they contain is important for every Christian, no matter when they live.

Revelation

The book of Revelation is quite different from anything else in the New Testament. It is mainly about visions which the author had. Some of them are quite difficult to understand because they are written in a sort of code. The book was written to encourage Christians who were being persecuted.

Summing up

The Bible is made up of many different books, but Christians believe they all contain important teachings.

Activities

A **1** What is a Covenant?

2 Why do the Gospels have this name? What is the difference between a Gospel and a life-story?

B **3** Explain why the two parts of the Bible are called the Old and New Testaments.

4 Why do Christian beliefs about the Old Testament differ from what Jews believe about it?

5 The word Gospels means 'good news'. Why do you think the men who wrote them used this title for their work?

C **6** Work with a partner or in a group to choose a story from either the Old Testament or the New Testament. (You could use a Bible or some of the units in this books to help you.) Write your own version of the story, and illustrate it.

25 The Creation story

The account of how the world began – the **Creation** – begins the book of Genesis, the first book of the Bible. Of all the stories in the Bible, this one probably causes most discussion, and most disagreement. Different Christians have very different ideas about it. Some Christians believe that every word is literally true. Some Christians believe that the whole thing is just a story, made up to explain things that people in those days could not understand. They feel the story has no meaning for us because we live in an age where science can explain many things that have puzzled people for centuries. Other Christians believe something between the two. They believe that the story is not a true account of what happened, and was not written to be 'believed in'. It was written as a story, but it teaches important lessons about human beings and God, and as such it still has meaning for people today.

What lessons might the story of Creation teach?

The most important lesson the story can teach is that the world is not an accident. God is the Creator, and is in control. God made everything, and was pleased with everything that he made. The high point of the Creation was the making of human beings, who were made to be like God and who were put in charge of everything else that God had made.

The Creation

The Bible's account does not try to explain *why* anything happened; it is a straightforward account of what the writer says happened. This is that God created the universe. There were eight acts of creation, which took place over six days. Each one began with the words: 'Then God commanded…' and ends with the words '…and God was pleased with what he saw'.

Christians believe God created the universe

Day 1 light and dark, and day and night

Day 2 earth's atmosphere ('a dome over the earth')

Day 3 dry land divided from the seas, plants on dry land

Day 4 sun, moon and stars, and therefore days, seasons and years

Day 5 sea creatures and birds

Day 6 land animals and people

Day 7 creation was finished, and God rested

The Fall

The Bible goes on to say that God gave the first people, Adam and Eve, a beautiful garden to live in. They were free to do anything they wished, except eat the fruit of one of the trees in the garden, the tree of knowledge. But the serpent, who was 'the most cunning animal that God had made' tempted Eve, and she ate the fruit from the tree of knowledge. Then she gave some to Adam.

God was angry, and he turned Adam and Eve out of the garden, saying:

> *'Because of what you have done, the ground will be under a curse. You will have to work hard all your life to make it produce enough food for you. It will produce weeds and thorns and you will have to eat wild plants. You will have to work hard and sweat to make the soil produce anything, until you go back to the soil from which you were formed.'*
>
> Genesis 3, 17–19

Why is the story so important for Christians?

Christians call this story 'the Fall', because it is the story of how Adam and Eve fell out of favour with God. The story teaches that God still cared for human beings, but their disobedience was a sin. A God who is holy cannot live with sin, so human beings had to be cut off from God. For Christians, this story connects directly to the story of Jesus. It explains why they believe that the death of Jesus was so important. The way to God, which had been closed by Adam and Eve, could only be reopened by the death of Jesus, God's son.

A well-dressing in Derbyshire

Summing up

The story of Creation and the Fall is one that is very important for Christians, even though there are disagreements about how it should be understood.

Activities

A

1 Why do Christians call the story of how Adam and Eve were thrown out of the garden 'the Fall'?

2 Explain why Christians believe that the story of the Fall connects with the life of Jesus.

B

3 The account in the Bible of the Creation is seen in different ways by different Christians. What are the main ways? What do you think is the best way to look at the story?

4 Explain why, according to the Bible, creating human beings was the high point of God's Creation. Do you think the world today shows this to be true?

5 What does the story of the Fall teach Christians? Why is the story so important for Christians?

C

6 Read the story of the Creation and the Fall in the Bible (Genesis chapters 1, 2 and 3). Write a brief account of what the Bible says, in your own words.

26 Baptism

Baptism (sometimes called Christening) is the special ceremony when people join the Church. In most Churches, baptism is the service in which a baby is officially given its name. Christians believe that it is a ceremony that washes away sin. This does not just mean things that a person has done wrong – obviously a baby has never done anything wrong. It includes all the things that come between people and God. So it is a symbol of the spiritual birth of the person.

Baptism is usually part of a normal church service. As well as the baby and its parents, family and friends come, too. Two or three friends or relations have the special role of being **godparents**. In some Churches, they are called sponsors. They promise that they will help the parents to bring the child up to follow Jesus. The parents make promises, answering questions from the vicar or minister. The questions here are taken from the Methodist Church service, but they are similar in most Churches.

Baptism of a baby

- Will you provide for this your child a Christian home of love and faithfulness?
- Will you help *him* by your words, prayers and example to renounce all evil and to put *his* trust in Jesus Christ as *his* Saviour?
- Will you encourage *him* to enter into full membership of the Church, and to serve Christ in the world?

To each question, the parents answer, 'With God's help, we will'.

At the beginning of the ceremony, everyone gathers around the font, which contains water that has been blessed. The baby is usually carried by one of the godparents. After the promises, the vicar or minister takes the baby in his or her arms, and uses the water to make the sign of the cross on the baby's forehead. As they do so, they say: 'I baptize you (*baby's name*) in the name of the Father, and of the Son and of the Holy Spirit.'

Total immersion baptism

Several Churches do not baptize babies. They have a service of blessing rather than baptism. This is because these Churches teach that anyone who is baptized should be old enough to understand why it is important, and be able to make the promises for themselves. Baptism services in these Churches usually take place when the person is in his or her teens. They are baptized by total immersion. This means that their whole body is placed under the water. In most Churches that baptize in this way, part of the floor can be made into a **baptistry**, a special waist-deep 'tank'. Sometimes a local swimming pool or river is used instead.

Before the person is baptized, they receive teaching about Christianity. For the service, men wear a white shirt and trousers,

Baptism by total immersion

women wear a long white dress. The minister often wears waders. The person who is being baptized walks down a short flight of steps into the water, and promises that they are sorry for the things they have done wrong in the past, and that they believe in Jesus. The minister then lowers them gently backwards under the water for a few seconds. This is a symbol that all their sins are being totally washed away. The person then leaves the pool, usually by a set of steps at the opposite end from where they entered it. This is to show that they are starting a new life with Jesus.

Baptism in the Orthodox Churches

Orthodox Churches usually baptize babies, but adults who are becoming Orthodox Christians are baptized too. Orthodox Churches always baptize by total immersion. The first part of the service takes place at the back of the church, with prayers to drive out all forms of evil from the person. The second part takes place at the font, and uses both oil and water. The priest says, 'The servant of God (*name*) is baptized into the Name of the Father, Amen. And of the Son, Amen. And of the Holy Spirit, Amen.' As each part of the Trinity is mentioned, the baby is immersed under the water. If the church does not have a baptistry, an adult who could not be immersed in a font may be baptized in a river, or a larger container would be used.

Immediately after the baptism with water, the person is **Chrismated**. The priest takes a special ointment and makes the sign of the cross on the person's forehead, eyes, nostrils, mouth, ears, chest, hands and feet. Each time, he says, 'The seal of the gift of the Holy Spirit.' After Chrismation, the baby or adult is counted as a full member of the Church, and receives Communion.

Summing up

Baptism is an important ceremony in most Churches. It marks the spiritual birth of the person as a Christian.

Activities

A

1. What is total immersion baptism? How is it different from other baptisms?
2. What do Christians believe that baptism symbolizes?

B

3. In some Churches, the water used for baptism comes from the River Jordan. Why do you think some Christians feel this is important?
4. Explain what the parents and godparents promise at an infant baptism.
5. What happens during Chrismation in the Orthodox Churches? Why is this important?

C

6. Work in pairs or small groups to discuss what sort of things could be called 'sin' – things that Christians believe can separate people from God.

27 Confirmation

Confirmation is a service held in Churches that baptize babies. It gives people a chance to make again ('confirm') for themselves the promises that were made on their behalf when they were baptized. Christians believe that at confirmation the person receives the Holy Spirit and becomes a full member of the Church. In some Churches, people do not receive the bread and wine at Communion until they have been confirmed.

In the Roman Catholic Church, **confirmands** are usually seven or eight years old, and the service is called First Communion. In most other Churches, confirmands are at least in their teens, but there is no age limit. In the Roman Catholic and Anglican Churches, confirmation is performed by a bishop. In other Churches, the service (which may have a different name) is carried out by the usual church minister.

Each confirmand is asked questions about what they believe. Then they make promises about their wish to follow the teachings of Jesus. The bishop lays his hands on their head, and prays for them. In the Roman Catholic Church, the bishop makes the sign of the cross with oil on the person's forehead. In most Churches, the newly confirmed person is given a Bible or service book, as a symbol to show that they are now a full member of the Church.

This account of how and why she became a member of the Methodist Church was written by Tanya, who is seventeen.

'Believing in anything these days is difficult. A football team, for instance, will not always win, and people will not always agree with your choice. When you tell people that you go to Church, some people think you're not normal. You can't be a normal teenager and go to Church! But why not? To be a Christian doesn't mean you can't be a normal teenager or a normal person in their twenties, thirties or whatever! I am not a "goody-goody-two-shoes". I don't force my faith on other people, but if someone asks me about it, I'm not ashamed to tell them what I believe and why. I don't have explanations or answers for everything, and I don't claim I have. All I know is what I do and don't believe.

A Roman Catholic confirmation service

'I have found being a Christian is fun, and unlike the way the media portray us, we are not all cult followers, or boring people who never laugh. I don't actually sit and watch *Songs of Praise*. Other people might like it, but I find it boring, and to me that's not what being a Christian is all about. I became a member of my Church because I enjoy going there, get a lot out of it and I like it. Someone else might like going to a drama club or a sports club, but Church is about slightly more important things than scoring goals!

Tanya

'Becoming a member of my Church wasn't difficult. I went to a group talk every week, to get to know what it meant to become a member, and be told things about my Church – things I probably didn't know at the time. Then in the service at church one Sunday morning, I was called to the front. If you can imagine a five-minute wedding service, it was a bit like that. I said some words, the minister said some words, and I was presented with a Bible.

'All my friends and family were there, it was really good. I didn't get dunked in water or have to say loads of prayers. Other Churches might do this, but ours isn't like that. All the denominations in the Church are different in the way they do things, so that you can find one which is suitable for you. It's a bit like choosing a car! Well, maybe not, because a car might break down or rust, but I believe God is always there. If you believe in him, you'll be driving shining Jags or Ferraris around in the life after death!'

Summing up

Confirmation is an important service for people who want to make their own commitment to Christianity.

Activities

A

1 What do you do if you confirm something? Why does this explain the purpose of a confirmation?

2 Who carries out confirmation services?

B

3 What age do you think someone should be before they are old enough to make serious promises for themselves?

4 Why do you think confirmands are given a Bible or a service book at the service?

5 What reasons can you think of why some Churches say that only people who have been confirmed should receive the bread and wine at Communion?

C

6 Write an account of a service of confirmation. If you have been to one, you could write about what happened. If not, use the information here plus anything else you can find out.

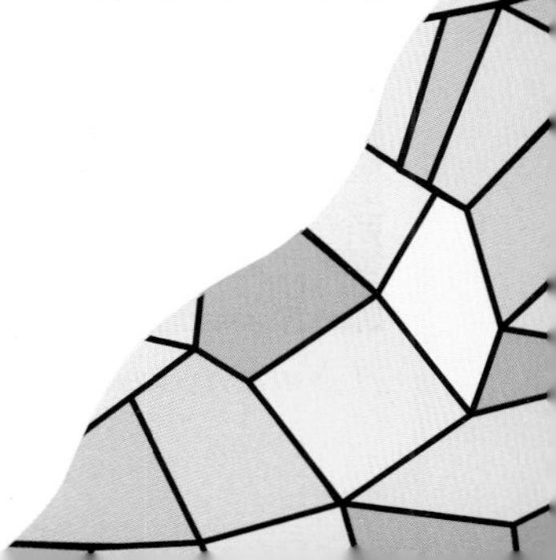

28 Festivals – Christmas

Christmas is now a national holiday in many parts of the world. Especially in rich countries like Britain, many people think that Christmas is about spending large amounts of money on presents, and eating and drinking far too much. It is a holiday and special time for people who have no religious beliefs at all. Many of the things that people think of as being part of 'Christmas' – trees, roast turkey, Father Christmas – have lost any religious meaning they might once have had. This does not mean that Christians do not take part in them. But for Christians, the real meaning of Christmas is far more important. It is to celebrate the birth of Jesus, who they believe was God's gift to the world.

Advent

Advent is a time of preparation for Christmas. It takes place during the four weeks of December. Christians look forward to celebrating the birth of Jesus, but they also remember that Jesus promised to come to earth again, to begin a new kingdom. The fact that it is a time of preparation is the reason why Advent calendars and candles are used. The candles are marked into 24 sections so that one section can be burned each day. Advent calendars usually have a door to open each day. Both calendars and candles emphasise that Christmas is getting closer.

A Nativity scene in a garden in Yorkshire

Why 25 December?

For about 300 years, nobody celebrated Jesus' birthday at all, because they did not know when it was. In those days, people did not keep such records. When Christians began to celebrate it, they chose a date that was already special. At that time, 25 December was the shortest day of the year. For hundreds of years, people believed that the sun was dying, and needed prayers and sacrifice to persuade it to return to give them another summer. The date 25 December was a religious festival, but it was also a holiday, when people gave each other presents and had a good time. For Christians who believed that God made everything, including the sun, it was an easy step to remember the Son of God on this day. It was also much easier to change the meaning of the festival than it would have been to try to stop people celebrating it altogether. Today, the calendar is different and the shortest day of the year is 21 December, but Christmas is still celebrated by most Christians on 25 December. The Orthodox Churches celebrate Christmas on 6 January, because of changes that were made to the Western calendar in the sixteenth century.

Christmas

'Christ's Mass' was originally the church service held to celebrate the birth of Jesus Christ on 25 December. Many Christians still think of Midnight Mass on Christmas Eve as being the most important service of the Christmas season. Christians usually make a special effort to go to church either for this service or for a service on Christmas morning. They want to thank God for giving his son Jesus to the world. The services include Bible readings about the birth of Jesus, and special songs called **carols**. Originally a carol was a dance and people used to dance around the church while they were singing.

Children often take part in Nativity plays

Boxing Day

Boxing Day is on 26 December. It is St Stephen's Day. Saint Stephen was the first Christian to die because of what he believed about Jesus, so he was given the honour of being remembered on the day after Jesus' birthday. Hundreds of years ago, money was distributed on this day. It had been collected in boxes in churches during the year, and on Boxing Day the boxes were opened and the money given to the poor. In the days when there was no 'social security' or other help for poor people, this was very important.

Epiphany

Epiphany comes from a Greek word which means 'to show'. It is the last part of the Church season of Christmas. In the Western Churches, it is celebrated on 6 January, and remembers how the child Jesus was shown to the wise men who had come to visit him. In the Orthodox Churches, it is celebrated on 19 January, and remembers Jesus' baptism, when he was shown to be the Son of God.

Summing up

Christmas is an important festival for all Christians.

Activities

A

1. Why do Christians use Advent calendars and candles?
2. What does Epiphany mean? What two things does it celebrate?

B

3. Why is Christmas celebrated on 25 December in the Western Church?
4. Where does the name Christmas come from? What does this tell you about the importance of the service?
5. No one today collects money to give to the poor on Boxing Day. What are the main ways in which Christians can help other people today? What do you think is the best way of helping people who are less fortunate than you?

C

6. Write your own poem, which could be used as a carol. Remember that carols are used for Advent and Epiphany as well as for Christmas.

29 Festivals – Easter

Easter is the time when Christians remember the death and Resurrection of Jesus. They prepare for it carefully, because it is the most important Christian festival.

Lent

Lent is the six weeks before Easter, and is the most solemn time of the Christian year. Christians remember the time that Jesus spent in the desert thinking about the work that God wanted him to do. Christians use the weeks of Lent to think about their lives. Many Christians spend more time reading the Bible and there are often special talks to discuss some part of Christian teaching.

The day before Lent begins is called Shrove Tuesday. In olden days, everyone went to Confession on this day, so that they could begin the solemn time of Lent free from sin. Shrove comes from an old word which means 'to be forgiven'. It is still a special day for Confession in some Churches. The other name for the day is Pancake Day. Lent used to be a time for fasting. Many Christians still give something up for Lent, and in the Orthodox Churches it is still a time of strict fasting. Pancakes were a traditional way of using up rich foods that would go off during the following six weeks, when people would not be eating them.

The first day of Lent is Ash Wednesday. Its name comes from the Church service held on this day, when special ash is used to make the sign of the cross on a person's forehead. It is a very serious service, when people say that they are really sorry for all the things they have done wrong, and promise to live better lives in the future. For many Christians this is still an important service, though it is not now held in all Churches.

Easter

The last week of Lent is called Holy Week, when Christians remember the last week of Jesus' life. It begins on Palm Sunday, when Christians remember Jesus riding into Jerusalem. The day on which they remember Jesus eating the Last Supper with the disciples is called Maundy Thursday. This comes from the Latin word *mandatum*, which means commandment. At the meal, Jesus told his friends that he was giving them a new commandment, to love one another.

On Good Friday, Christians remember the crucifixion. There are often solemn church services, especially in the afternoon, as the Bible says that Jesus died at three o'clock. Churches never have flowers or decorations on this day. The name *Good* Friday seems odd for the day on which Jesus died, but it shows what Christians believe Jesus' death did for people. For Christians, Jesus' death opened up the way to God, and means that everyone's sins can be forgiven.

A 'Passion play' retells the Easter story

An Orthodox service at Easter

Easter Sunday is the most joyful day of the Christian year. Christians celebrate their belief that Jesus came back to life, and is still alive today. Churches are decorated and there are often early morning Eucharist services. In the Orthodox Churches, a special service is held at midnight as Easter Day begins. The church is in darkness, to show that Jesus is in the tomb. (One of the titles that Christians give Jesus is the Light of the World.) Then the priest comes out from behind the centre screen with a lighted candle, and all the people light their candles from his. Light fills the church. The priest calls, 'Christ is Risen!' and the people answer, 'He is risen indeed'. In some countries, it is the custom to light bonfires and set off fireworks, and spend the night feasting and rejoicing.

Summing up

Easter is a time of great joy for all Christians.

Activities

A 1 What two names are given to the day before Lent begins? Explain where the names come from.

2 Where does the name 'Maundy' come from?

B 3 Why do you think Easter is a more important festival for Christians than Christmas?

4 During Lent, many Christians give up a luxury. Why do you think they do this?

5 Explain as carefully as you can why Christians call the day on which Jesus died 'Good Friday'.

C 6 Find out as much as you can about the special service that is held on Maundy Thursday when the Queen gives out 'Maundy money'. Prepare a talk that you could give to the rest of your group.

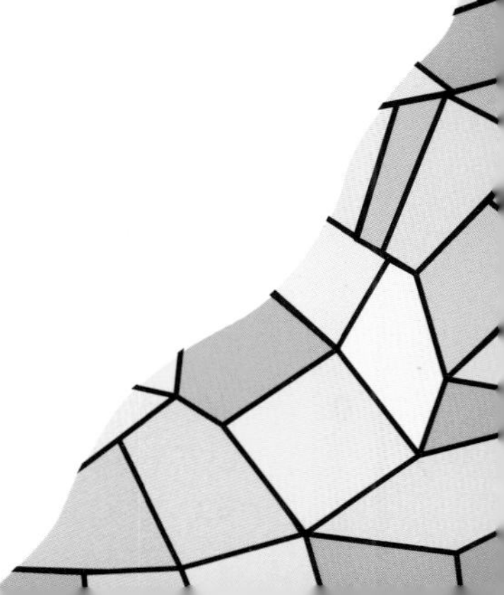

Important places in Christianity

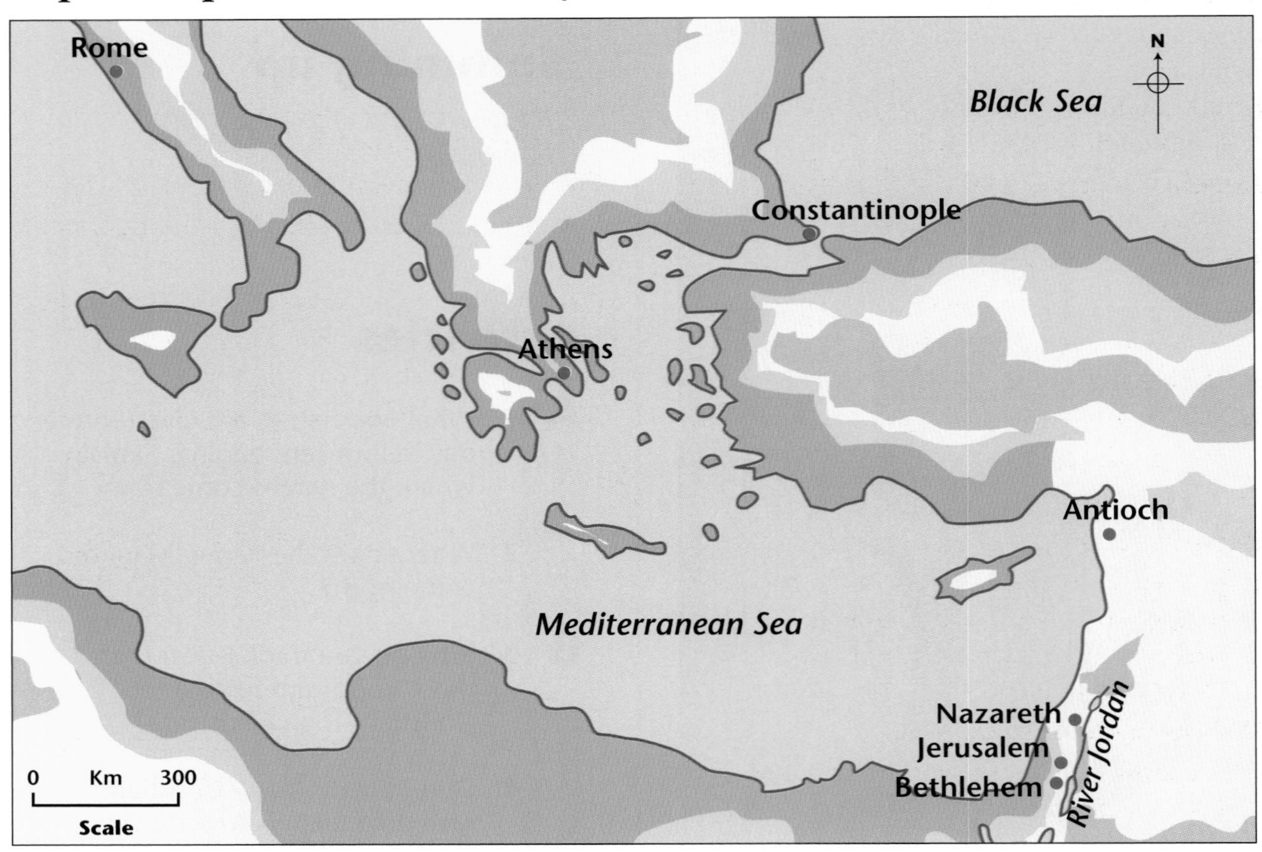

Time chart

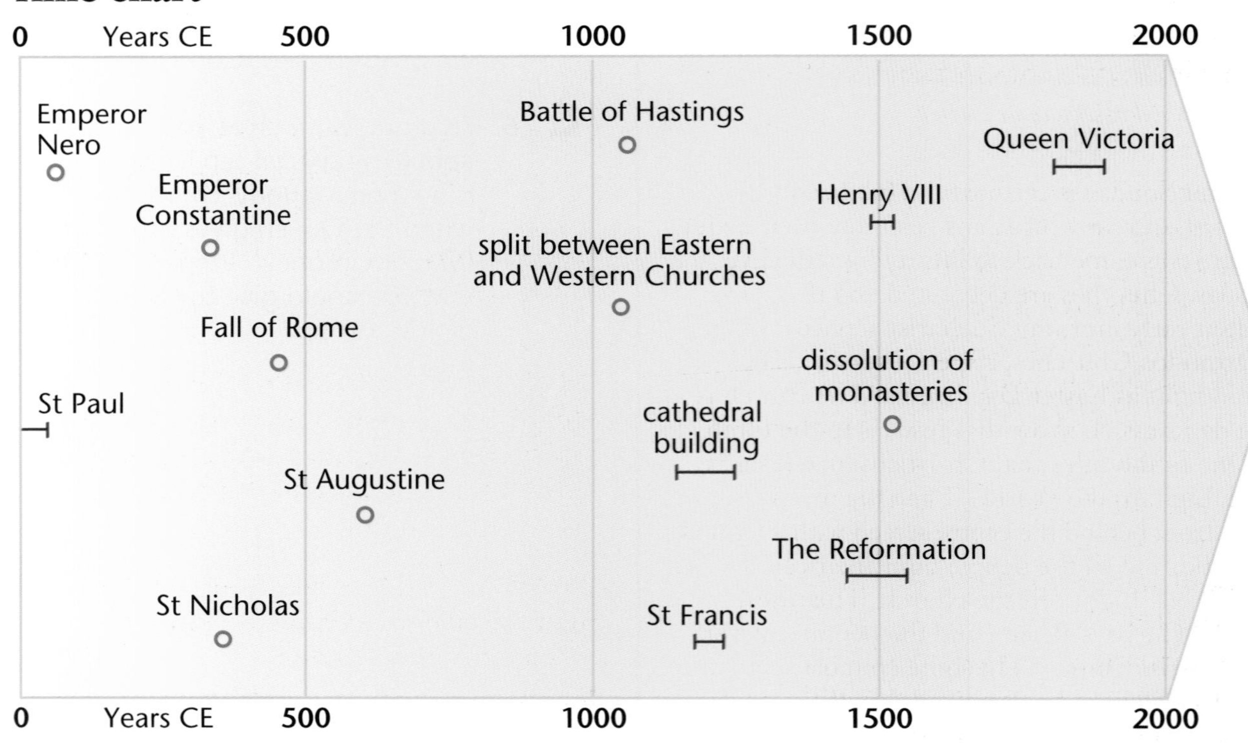

Glossary

Altar a table used for the service of Holy Communion

Angelus a prayer to the Virgin Mary – also called Ave Maria or Hail Mary

Anoint to rub with oil

Apostle 'one who is sent out' – name given to some of the first followers of Jesus

Archbishop a senior bishop

Ascension the last occasion on which Jesus met his disciples

Baptism a special ceremony to wash away sin

Baptistry a special small rectangular pool, with steps at both ends, that can be filled with water for Christians to be baptized by total immersion

Bishop a senior priest

Blasphemy saying something that shows disrespect for God

Cardinals senior men in the Roman Catholic Church, responsible for electing the Pope

Carols joyful songs to celebrate Christmas (and Easter)

Cathedra a bishop's throne

Cathedral a church which houses a bishop's throne

Chrismation part of the baptism ceremony in Orthodox Churches

Christ the title given by Christians to Jesus (it means Messiah)

Clergy men or women who have been ordained

Confession admitting the things you have done wrong

Confirmands people who are being confirmed

Confirmation service at which someone becomes a full member of their Church

Covenant a solemn agreement

Creation the account in the Bible of the beginning of the world

Creed a statement of belief

Crucifix a cross that includes the figure of Jesus

Crucifixion method of killing someone by nailing or tying them to a cross and leaving them to die

Crucify to kill by nailing or tying someone to a cross

Denomination a branch of Christianity

Disciple 'someone who learns' – follower of Jesus

Eternal without beginning or end

Eucharist 'thanksgiving' – another name for the service of Holy Communion

Fast not eating or drinking anything, for religious reasons

Font a special bowl used to hold the water for baptism

Gentile anyone who is not a Jew

Godparents friends or relatives who take part in a baptism service

Gospels the four books in the Bible which tell of Jesus' life

Hebrew the language of the Jews

Holy Communion the most important Christian service, remembering the last meal Jesus ate with his disciples

Incense sweet smelling spices for burning

Icon a religious painting of Jesus, the Virgin Mary or a saint

Iconostasis the screen which divides an Orthodox church

Judaism the religion of the Jews

Liturgy the service of Holy Communion in Orthodox Churches

Mass the Roman Catholic service of Holy Communion

Messiah one sent by God to free the Jews

Minister a member of the clergy in the Free Churches

Ministry time spent preaching and teaching

Miracle an event that cannot be explained, but which shows God's power

Missal a Roman Catholic service book

Monks men who have chosen to dedicate their lives to God

Monotheism the belief that there is only one God

Nave the main part of a church

Ordained 'set apart' – a person who has been made a member of the clergy

Orthodox the eastern Churches, mainly based in Greece and Russia

Parable a story with a meaning

Parish a local area

Patriarchs leaders of the Orthodox Churches

Persecution punishment for what you believe

Pharisees Jewish religious leaders at the time of Jesus

Pope the head of the Roman Catholic Church

Priest a member of the clergy (often Roman Catholic, but the title is used by other Churches, too)

Prophets men and women who were messengers from God

Protestant a Christian who is neither Orthodox nor Roman Catholic

Psalm a special poem from the Bible used in worship

Rector a member of the Anglican clergy

Repent to show that you are sorry for things you have done wrong

Resurrection the Christian belief that Jesus rose from the dead

Roman Catholic a member of the Church that has the Pope as its head

Sabbath the Jewish day of rest and worship (Saturday)

Sacrifice killing an animal so that its life can be given to God

Saint someone who was especially close to God when he or she was alive

Sanctuary 'holy place' – the part of a church nearest the altar

Sanhedrin the highest Jewish court

Sermon a talk which is part of a church service

Sins wrong-doing – everything that cuts people off from God

Spirit a being which exists but does not have a physical body

Symbol something that stands for something else

Temple the most important building in the Jewish religion

Testament 'agreement' – part of the Bible

Total immersion baptism baptism where the whole body is placed under water

Trinity the belief that there is only one God, but he can be seen in three ways – Father, Son and Holy Spirit

Vicar a member of the Anglican clergy

Worship to show respect and love for God